AAT

Work Effectively in Finance

Level 2
Foundation Certificate in
Accounting
Course Book

Third edition 2018

ISBN 9781 5097 1821 4
ISBN (for internal use only) 9781 5097 1817 7

British Library Cataloguing-in-Publication Data
A catalogue record for this book is available from the British Library

Published by

BPP Learning Media Ltd
BPP House, Aldine Place
142-144 Uxbridge Road
London W12 8AA

www.bpp.com/learningmedia

Printed in the United Kingdom

BPP
LEARNING MEDIA

Contents

Introduction to the course

Syllabus overview

This unit helps students to develop professional skills and behaviours needed in the workplace. The unit is set in the context of an accounting function, however, skills gained are transferable to many other working environments.

Students will:

- Understand the work of the finance function and why that work is important to an organisation

- Understand the skills required of finance employees, including social skills, communication skills and essential numeracy skills

- Learn the importance of being an effective employee and working as part of a team

- Be able to identify activities that develop current skills and knowledge, and those that will help them achieve future career aspirations

- Understand how to ensure data security and the importance of maintaining confidentiality of information

- Understand the importance of corporate social responsibility and the actions that can be taken to ensure corporations behave ethically and support sustainability

Test specification for this unit assessment

Assessment method	Marking type	Duration of assessment
Computer based synoptic assessment	Partially computer/ partially human marked	2 hours

Learning outcomes
1 Understand the finance function within an organisation
2 Use personal skills development in finance
3 Produce work effectively
4 Understand corporate social responsibility (CSR) within organisations

Synoptic assessment outcomes	Weighting
1 Demonstrate an understanding of the finance function and the roles and procedures carried out by members of an accounting team	24%
2 Process transactions, complete calculations and make journal entries	24%
3 Compare, produce and reconcile journals and accounts	34%
4 Communicate financial information effectively	18%
Total	**100%**

Assessment structure

2 hours duration

Competency is 70%

*Note that this is only a guideline as to what might come up. The format and content of each task may vary from what we have listed below.

Your assessment will consist of 7 tasks.

Task	Expected content	Max marks	Unit ref	Study complete
Task 1	**Plan workload to meet the needs of the organisation** Preparation of a to do list comprising routine and ad hoc tasks for one or more finance functions. Information can be given in a variety of forms for this task, and may include pop-up windows listing normal work schedules. A bookkeeping task from the above schedule may be selected for completion. An example of this may be entering receipts and payments into a two column analysed cash book, followed by the totalling and balancing of this cash book. Similarly, this task could relate to entering receipts and payments into an analysed petty cash book.	12	Work effectively in finance Bookkeeping transactions	

Task	Expected content	Max marks	Unit ref	Study complete
Task 2	**Understanding the finance function within an organisation** This task may overlap with other learning outcomes, for example by requiring compilation of a list of items within a form of communication. The list of items could be: Roles of the finance function Types of information received from stakeholders Types of information provided by the finance function The importance of ensuring data security Characteristics of useful information How to maintain solvency How to ensure legal or regulatory compliance Policies or procedures to be familiar with The form of communication may be: A memo/An email/A letter **Using personal skills development in finance** Another element of this task can require personal skills to be identified, and may include: Interpersonal skills, listening skills, business language, body language Effective team characteristics, team roles (Belbin), and actions contributing to teamwork The importance of CPD, and activities relevant to CPD	12	Work effectively in finance	

Task	Expected content	Max marks	Unit ref	Study complete
Task 3	**Processing customer transactions or Processing supplier transactions**	12	Bookkeeping transactions	
	This task may require the completion of a sales invoice (or credit note), and including:			
	Finding and applying relevant quantities, prices and codes from pop-up lists or scenarios			
	Calculating trade discount, net, VAT and total amounts			
	Calculating settlement discounts, and deciding when they are applicable			
	The task may, alternately, require the checking of the accuracy of purchase invoices (or credit notes) and deciding on payment amounts after settlement discount.			

Task	Expected content	Max marks	Unit ref	Study complete
Task 4	**Process transactions through the ledgers to the trial balance** **Use control accounts** This task may require understanding of a day book (purchase or sales), and using it to transfer data to a control account (purchase ledger or sales ledger). A partially completed control account may be provided and the student asked to calculate balances carried down. This task may be extended to feature the subsidiary ledger (purchase or sales), enabling the student to calculate a difference between the subsidiary ledger and the relevant control account, as well as identifying possible reasons for the difference. **Produce accurate work in appropriate formats** A further part to the task may provide a form of written communication (email, letter) linked to the above scenario, and requiring the student to identify spelling and grammar errors. This written communication will be human marked.	16	Bookkeeping transactions Bookkeeping controls Work effectively in finance	

Task	Expected content	Max marks	Unit ref	Study complete
Task 5	**Understand corporate social responsibility (CSR) within an organisation** Within this task the student may be asked to identify CSR or sustainability initiatives. Alternately students may be given scenarios highlighting ethical issues, and required to identify appropriate course of action for individuals concerned. **Provide information on actual and budgeted costs and income** Linked to the above scenario, students may be required to process costing data to enable decision making. An example of this may be the provision of a cost performance report where budget or actual figures need to be calculated and inserted in a table, leading to the calculation of variances.	12	Work effectively in finance Elements of costing	

Task	Expected content	Max marks	Unit ref	Study complete
Task 6	**Use cost recording techniques** This task may use any cost recording techniques within Learning outcome 2. As an example a scenario may provide data to enable a table of fixed, variable, total and unit costs to be calculated for different levels of output. **Produce accurate work in appropriate formats** The student may be required to write (type) a short, structured report on a feature of the above scenario and data, for example: Defining terms, such as fixed costs Providing an analysis of the data This written report will be human marked.	24	Elements of costing Work effectively in finance	
Task 7	**Transfer data from the books of prime entry to the ledgers** This task may provide an extract of a daybook (purchase or sales) and require the student to transfer data to the ledger accounts in the general and subsidiary ledgers **Use the journal** The latter part of the task may provide information on an error in the general ledger and require completion of a journal. This or another journal may then be required to be posted to the general ledger accounts.	12	Bookkeeping transactions Bookkeeping controls	

Skills bank

Our experience of preparing students for this type of assessment suggests that to obtain competency, you will need to develop a number of key skills.

What do I need to know to do well in the assessment?

Work Effectively in Finance (WEFN) is part of the mandatory Level 2 synoptic assessment (FSYA). This assessment also includes significant elements of other Level 2 units: Bookkeeping Transactions, Bookkeeping Controls and Elements of Costing, for which you should refer to the relevant Course Books, as well as practice assessments in the Level 2 FSYA Question Bank.

To be successful in the assessment you need to:

- Understand the finance function within an organisation (including roles and data security)

- Be able to develop personal skills in finance (interpersonal and teamwork skills, Continuing Professional Development)

- Be able to produce work effectively (involving communication, presentation and self-organisation)

- Understand Corporate Social Responsibility within an organisation (including ethics and sustainability)

Assumed knowledge

There is no assumed knowledge within this unit, which covers many of the non-accounting skills required in an office environment, other than basic literacy and numeracy.

Assessment style

For the WEFN part of the synoptic assessment you will complete tasks by:

1   Entering narrative by selecting from drop down menus of narrative options known as **picklists**

2   Using **drag and drop** menus to enter narrative

3   Typing in numbers, known as **gapfill** entry

4   Entering **ticks**

5   Entering **dates** by selecting from a calendar

6   **Written** answers

You must familiarise yourself with the style of the online questions and the AAT software before taking the synoptic assessment. As part of your revision, login to the **AAT website** and attempt their **online practice assessments**.

Answering written questions

In your assessment there will be written questions and these may be in the form of preparing notes for management meetings or preparing brief reports for colleagues. The main verbs used for these types of question requirements, are as follows, along with their meaning:

Identify – Analyse and select for presentation

Explain – Set out in detail the meaning of

Discuss – by argument, discuss the pros and cons

Analysing the scenario

Before answering the question set, you need to carefully review the scenario given in order to consider what questions need to be answered, and what needs to be discussed. A simple framework that could be used to answer the question is as follows:

- Point – make the point
- Evidence – use the information from the scenario as evidence
- Explain – explain why the evidence links to the point

For example, if an assessment task asked us to explain how fixed costs behave we could answer as follows:

1   Point – fixed costs are expected to remain the same over all levels of output

2   Evidence – fixed costs have remained constant even though output has increased over the last three months

3   Explain – this means that the fixed cost per unit will decrease as output increases

Recommendations can also be required, and are to provide guidance on how to proceed. If fixed costs had increased without explanation then:

1   Recommendation – the unexplained increase in fixed costs should be reported to management so this increase can be investigated

This approach provides a formula or framework that can be followed to answer written questions:

Fixed costs are expected to remain the same (Point)....output has increased (Evidence)....fixed cost per unit will decrease (Explain)

If a recommendation is required:

Report to management (Recommendation).

Introduction to the assessment

The question practice you do will prepare you for the format of tasks you will see in the *Work Effectively in Finance* part of the synoptic assessment. It is also useful to familiarise yourself with the introductory information you **may** be given at the start of the assessment. For example:

Each task is independent. You will not need to refer to your answers to previous tasks.

Read every task carefully to make sure you understand what is required.

Where the date is relevant, it is given in the task data.

Read the scenario carefully before attempting the questions, you can return to it at any time by clicking on the 'introduction' button at the bottom of the screen.

Complete all 7 tasks.

Answer the questions in the spaces provided. For answers requiring free text entry, the box will expand to fit your answer.

You must use a full stop to indicate a decimal point. For example, write 100.57 NOT 100,57 OR 100 57.

Both minus signs and brackets can be used to indicate negative numbers unless task instructions say otherwise.

You may use a comma to indicate a number in the thousands, but you don't have to. For example, 10000 and 10,000 are both acceptable.

Where the date is relevant, it is given in the task data.

Information

- The total time for this paper is 2 hours.
- This assessment has a total of 7 tasks which are divided into subtasks.
- The total mark for this paper is 100.
- The marks for each sub-task are shown alongside the task.

1   As you revise, use the **BPP Passcards** to consolidate your knowledge. They are a pocket-sized revision tool, perfect for packing in that last-minute revision.

2   Attempt as many tasks as possible in the **Level 2 FSYA Question Bank**. There are plenty of assessment-style tasks which are excellent preparation for the real assessment.

3   Always **check** through your own answers as you will in the real assessment, before looking at the solutions in the back of the Question Bank.

Key to icons

Key term — A key definition which is important to be aware of for the assessment

Formula to learn — A formula you will need to learn as it will not be provided in the assessment

Formula provided — A formula which is provided within the assessment and generally available as a pop-up on screen

Activity — An example which allows you to apply your knowledge to the technique covered in the Course Book. The solution is provided at the end of the chapter

Illustration — A worked example which can be used to review and see how an assessment question could be answered

Assessment focus point — A high priority point for the assessment

Open book reference — Where use of an open book will be allowed for the assessment

Real life examples — A practical real life scenario

AAT qualifications

The material in this book may support the following AAT qualifications:

AAT Foundation Certificate in Accounting Level 2, AAT Foundation Certificate in Accounting at SCQF Level 5 and AAT Foundation Diploma in Accounting and Business Level 2.

Supplements

From time to time we may need to publish supplementary materials to one of our titles. This can be for a variety of reasons, from a small change in the AAT unit guidance to new legislation coming into effect between editions.

You should check our supplements page regularly for anything that may affect your learning materials. All supplements are available free of charge on our supplements page on our website at:

www.bpp.com/learning-media/about/students

Improving material and removing errors

There is a constant need to update and enhance our study materials in line with both regulatory changes and new insights into the assessments.

From our team of authors BPP appoints a subject expert to update and improve these materials for each new edition.

Their updated draft is subsequently technically checked by another author and from time to time non-technically checked by a proof reader.

We are very keen to remove as many numerical errors and narrative typos as we can but given the volume of detailed information being changed in a short space of time we know that a few errors will sometimes get through our net.

We apologise in advance for any inconvenience that an error might cause. We continue to look for new ways to improve these study materials and would welcome your suggestions. Please feel free to contact our AAT Head of Programme at nisarahmed@bpp.com if you have any suggestions for us.

These learning materials are based on the qualification specification released by the AAT in April 2018.

The role of the financial functions

Learning outcomes

1.1	**Identify the role of the finance function**
	• The role of the finance function: responsibility for production of statutory financial statements, providing a service (information, support, advice and guidance) to both internal and external stakeholders

1.2	**Demonstrate an understanding of how finance staff contribute to an organisation's success**
	• The importance of establishing good business relationships
	• The principles of effective communication: content is written clearly, complete, accurate, timely, concise and meets the needs of the recipient, and an appropriate medium is used in a suitable environment
	• Actions of finance staff that support efficient working practices, solvency and long-term financial stability, legal and regulatory compliance
	• The importance to an organisation's survival of remaining solvent and managing funds effectively

1.3	**Indicate the role of information in the work of the finance function**
	• Types of information and documentation received by the finance function: budgetary, inventory control and costing information, information from suppliers and customers, purchase orders, remittance advice, statements, supplier invoices, credit notes
	• Types of information and documentation produced by the finance function: information to help management decision making, budgetary information, cash information, taxation information, information for suppliers and customers, sales invoices, credit notes, statements
	• The importance of providing useful information
	• Characteristics of useful information: complete, accurate, timely and fit for purpose.

Assessment context

The role of finance staff and the information produced by them is an important element of the unit syllabus, and is likely to be examined. Assessment tasks will seek to test knowledge and understanding of this operation. This may be done with a statement of a stakeholder need followed by a requirement to select, from various options, the relevant information to provide.

Qualification context

This chapter focuses on the primary roles of finance staff, and so is relevant to the start of the unit. The roles are to be understood in an overall way contributing to personal objectives. This naturally leads to discussion of more specific skills such as communication and teamwork.

Reference to these roles may be made occasionally in other units in Levels 3 and 4, but not examined specifically.

Business context

Understanding the finance role would usually be a part of induction to an organisation. It should give employees a sense of their personal objectives within an organisation, and so contribute to better productivity and efficiency.

Chapter overview

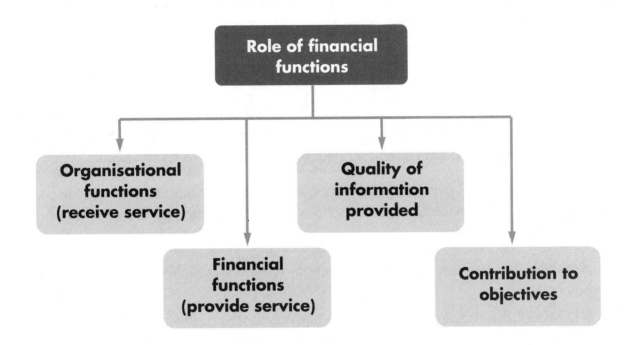

Introduction

In our first chapter we look at how the functions in an organisation can work together to meet organisational objectives. This can include not only making a profit, but also having a enough cash available to pay day to day expenses.

1 Stakeholders

All organisations, business or otherwise, have **stakeholders**, and a primary objective of a finance function is to provide information to, or receive information from, them. This makes it an important relationship, and one to be developed.

Key term

> **Stakeholders** can be anyone who has an interest in an organisation. They can be individuals, and are often other organisations, who are affected by the activities of the business.

The relationship between the finance function and the stakeholders can depend on whether they are:

(a) Internal stakeholders – who work within the same organisation (examples are employees in general, department managers, and other functions)

(b) External stakeholders – who do not work within the organisation (examples include customers, suppliers, banks, the local community and potential investors)

It is useful to imagine what interest each stakeholder has in an organisation, for example the employee who wants a stable company to provide them with a good source of income and job satisfaction.

2 Functions within an organisation

An organisation may perform a number of different activities in pursuit of its objectives, depending on what type of organisation it is. These activities may include:

- The research, design and development of products and services (R&D)

- Production (in a manufacturing organisation) or other operational activities (such as providing services)

- The marketing and selling of products or services to customers

- The development and use of information technology (IT) systems for the business

- The purchasing or procurement of materials and supplies used in the business

- The warehousing, transport and distribution of finished products (sometimes called 'logistics')

- The management of the organisation's staff or 'human resources' (HR) (sometimes referred to as personnel)

- Administrative and clerical activities supporting the running of the business

- The management of the organisation's finances and financial information (accounting and finance)

Some of these functions, known as **line functions**, are directly involved in the main service-delivering or revenue-earning activity of the business: they directly fulfil the organisation's primary purpose and objectives. Examples include the production, marketing, sales and distribution functions.

Other functions, known as **staff functions**, exist to support the line functions in fulfilling their objectives: providing them with the resources, systems and information they need to perform their activities efficiently and effectively. Examples include IT, HR (personnel), administration – and accounting and finance.

3 The financial functions

You may already have some grasp of the role and tasks of the accounting and payroll functions from your work, or from your studies for other units. However, it may be helpful to have an overview here, with a particular focus on how accounting and payroll 'fit' within the organisation as a whole.

3.1 The accounting function

The role of the accounting function generally is to support the organisation's other functions by compiling, preparing and providing complete, accurate and timely information on all financial aspects of the business. Business accounting is the process of:

- Recording all financial transactions carried out by an organisation
- Summarising the transactions to present a financial picture which supports both:
    - Accountability to investors and other external interested parties (or stakeholders); and
    - Internal management decision-making about the business.

This function is often split into other sub-functions.

3.2 Financial accounting

Financial accounting is mainly concerned with the processing and recording of transactions (bookkeeping), and the production of financial statements for users outside the business (external stakeholders).

The financial accounts function firstly records transactions between the business and its customers, suppliers, employees and owners. These records then enable any business of any size, from a 'one man band' sole trader to a large professional partnership or company, to prepare its financial statements:

- A statement of financial position or SOFP
- A statement of profit or loss or SPL
- Other primary financial statements and notes if required

Statutory financial statements for companies are required by law, in particular:

- To be presented in compliance with detailed regulations;

- To be audited, where necessary (to ensure that they represent a true and fair picture of the financial position of the company); and

- To be lodged with a government official called the Registrar of Companies, so that they can be made available to suppliers, investors and other interested parties.

Similarly, taxation records of all businesses must be compiled according to detailed rules, and submitted to HM Revenue & Customs.

3.3 Management accounting

Management accounting is mainly concerned with the production of financial reports to assist managers (internal stakeholders) in all the business's functions in:

- Measuring performance
- Making decisions
- Generally running the business

Management accounts are not regulated by law: managers can ask for whatever records and reports they think will be helpful to them. Unlike financial accounts, these are purely internal documents and, for commercial reasons, are mostly kept strictly confidential.

Management accountants perform activities such as cost analysis, cost control, budget preparation and budgetary control (monitoring actual performance against budgeted performance).

3.4 Information flows to and from the accounting function

The Accounts department needs to receive information from all the other departments of the organisation, in order to compile reports and records on the financial implications of their activities. Examples include cost estimates; production schedules; expenses claim forms; records of staff work and overtime hours (eg timesheets or clock cards); changes to staff details (eg pay grades, leave arrangements, promotions); invoices to process and pay; purchase orders and goods received notes to check against invoices – and so on.

In return, the Accounts department provides information to all the departments of the organisation on the financial implications of their activities: wage/salary costs; current costs against expected/budgeted costs; expenses; **cash flow** summaries; customer debts (for the Sales or Credit Control department); revenue and profit forecasts; and so on.

3.5 Payroll

The payroll function may be a section of the accounting function. It is concerned solely with payroll processing, including tasks such as: the calculation of gross pay from salary data and timesheets etc; the calculation of tax, National Insurance and other deductions; preparing payslips; making appropriate returns to external agencies such as HM Revenue & Customs; making up wage packets with cash, or preparing data for direct credit of salaries to employees' bank accounts (BACS); distributing payslips to employees; and preparing payroll statistics.

Activity 1: Payroll information

From what we have just said about the tasks performed by the payroll function, see if you can determine from the following list:

(a)   Information required by the Payroll department from the HR department and other departments where people are employed

(b)   Information provided by the Payroll department to other internal and external parties

Required

Tick the appropriate box.

Information	Required by payroll from other departments	Provided by payroll to other parties
Total wage/salary and overtime costs		
Employees' National Insurance details		
Date of commencement of employment		
Information for individual employees about pay and deductions		
Statutory returns to external agencies		
Standard and overtime hours worked		
Wage/salary and overtime rates		

3.6 Other financial functions

An organisation may have separate sections for other (or more specific) aspects of finance, such as:

- Cash administration and money-handling tasks, such as cashiers, petty cash and banking

- Financing (eg managing loans and other sources of finance)

- Taxation

4 The financial functions as service and support providers

It is important to realise that people in finance do not work in isolation, and need to foster good relationships with contacts. Whatever their specific tasks, the financial functions as a whole provide a service to all the other functions in the organisation, supporting them in the fulfilment of their objectives – and, through them, the objectives of the organisation as a whole. The 'customers' of the financial function include all of the other functions in the organisation.

4.1 Financial information

The main role of the accounting and payroll functions is to support managers and staff in other functions by preparing and providing complete, accurate and timely information on the financial implications of their activities.

The accounting function provides information about the financial implications of operational activities such as holding inventory and making sale and purchase transactions. The accounting function shows:

- What the activities cost (both immediately and over time);

- What revenues, returns or benefits they earn;

- What the balance is between cash coming into and cash going out of the business (**cash flow**); and

- What the cash flow situation means for:

    - The availability of day to day finance to maintain organisational activity (this is the **working capital** required by the business); and

    - The ability of the organisation to pay its debts when they fall due (its **solvency**).

For other functions of the organisation, this information highlights important decision factors such as:

- What they can afford to spend
- What they need to earn
- How profitable and efficient their activities are
- Where their profitability or **efficiency** may need to be improved

The payroll function similarly provides information about the financial implications of employing people:

- How much cash is needed to pay them

- How much it costs to keep the organisation staffed and operating

- Whether there is potential to increase – or a need to decrease – staffing or staff costs

Accounting information therefore supports managers in making sound decisions about the resources available to them. It equips managers for:

- **Planning**: helping them to understand the financial implications of their planned activities; what resources are or are not available to implement them (ie whether their planned activities are affordable); and their potential costs and benefits in financial terms (ie whether the planned activities are cost effective and worthwhile)

- **Control**: helping them to measure the results of their activities against their plans; whether they came in 'on budget' (in line with anticipated costs); whether they earned the expected revenues and profits; whether resources were efficiently used; and so on

4.2 Complete, accurate and timely information

In fulfilling this service role, the important thing for the finance function is not the quantity of information but its quality. In order to be of maximum benefit to the organisation, the information provided must be complete, accurate and timely:

- **Complete**: including all data relevant to the purpose for which the information will be used

- **Accurate**: factually and numerically correct, and to an appropriate level of detail for the purpose for which the information will be used

- **Timely**: delivered at the right time for the information to be meaningful and used to support decision making and action

5 Contribution to business objectives

We have looked at what the financial functions broadly 'do' within the business: that is, their role. But why is this important? What does it contribute to the fulfilment of business objectives and the success of the organisation as a whole?

By providing financial information to all functions and departments within an organisation, those in accounting, payroll and other financial roles make an important contribution in three key areas:

- The smooth running and efficiency of the business
- The working capital and solvency of the business
- The legal compliance of the business

5.1 Smooth running and efficiency

Information is the lifeblood of all business activity. The financial functions play an important role in the smooth running of the organisation, through supplying high-quality, timely information to support managers in their decision making.

Organisational efficiency is about achieving objectives with the minimum use of resources (particularly the minimum unnecessary expenditure or waste).

The financial functions support efficiency by providing information for planning (so that resources are not used thoughtlessly) and control (so that the use of resources is checked, and managers are held accountable for how they are used).

- In collaboration with other department managers, the accounting function produces annual budgets and long-term plans, which act as guidelines and benchmarks for measuring the performance of different departments, and the organisation as a whole.

- They periodically provide departments with information on how they are actually performing or progressing, for comparison against the benchmarks set out in plans and budgets.

- This enables departments to measure how effectively and efficiently they are operating, and to identify areas where performance and efficiency can be improved – or where forecasts and plans may need to be adjusted to be more realistic.

5.2 Working capital and solvency

The accounting function has a very important role in managing working capital: the day to day finance which is used to keep the business running. Working capital basically comprises:

Inventory		Payables	
Receivables	LESS	Overdrafts	
Cash			

The accounting function provides information to other departments about the cash flow implications of their activities: what money is flowing into the organisation and when (income) and what money is flowing out of the organisation and when (expenditure), and the balance between these two flows at any given time. The organisation and its various functions can then:

- Know what working capital is available for use at any given time

- Ensure there is an adequate cash balance at any given time by managing:

  - The level of inventory, by ensuring that no more is held than is necessary

  - The collection of receipts from receivables, by operating a strict credit control policy

  - The making of payments to payables, by negotiating favourable credit terms

- Plan to earn extra revenue, or to raise finance (eg by taking out a loan or selling assets), if required to maintain adequate reserves of working capital

By closely monitoring the cash balances of the business, the accounting function also has a very important role in ensuring the solvency of the organisation: that is, its ability to meet its short-term and long-term debts as they fall due.

The accounting function provides information to the organisation about:

- Debts that are owed to the organisation and when they are due to be paid by customers (receivables)

- The availability of cash to cover payables when they fall due

- The cost of raising finance (eg through share capital, loans and other means) to keep the organisation solvent

5.3 Legal compliance

The preparation of financial and payroll information and records is subject to complex legal and regulatory requirements.

It is yet another important role of the accounting and payroll functions to ensure that all legal and regulatory requirements are met. This helps the organisation:

- To benefit from a positive reputation and track record of financial integrity and legal compliance (which may, in turn, enable the organisation to attract and retain investors, customers, suppliers and high-quality staff)

- To avoid or minimise liabilities arising from non-compliance, including financial penalties (in the form of fines or even imprisonment); the cost of remedial work to bring records and returns into compliance; the loss of shareholder, share market and regulator confidence; and the burden of more onerous scrutiny in future

For your assessment, you won't be required to demonstrate knowledge of specific legislation. However, you will be expected to demonstrate an awareness that payroll and accounting staff are always required to follow the rules and procedures laid down by their organisation to ensure that working practices comply with legislative and regulatory requirements.

In order to ensure compliance, the organisation should:

- Make all employees aware of the importance of compliance

- Brief all employees on their roles and responsibilities under the law (and update the briefings as the law changes), from the induction of new recruits onwards

- Base organisational policies and procedures (and related employee training) on legal requirements

- Put in place checks and controls, to monitor and ensure compliance

Illustration 1: Supplying information

Southfield Electronics is a supplier of a wide range of consumer electronics appliances to specialist retailers and department stores.

The accounting function regularly supplies the Sales department with information including:

- Breakdowns of sales revenue by region – so that plans can be made to increase sales effort in underperforming regions (and reward the best-performing sales teams)

- Reports on the value of the inventory of goods held in the warehouse

- Reports on sales revenue to date (compared with budget) and cost of sales activity to date (compared with budget)

- Reports on the amounts owing by each retail customer, and when they fall due, highlighting overdue amounts

The accounting function supplies the Purchasing department with:

- Reports on expenditure to date (compared with budget) on bought-in materials and services for the organisation

- A list of discrepancies between supplier invoices and purchase orders – so that Purchasing can query this with suppliers

Recent information has highlighted two issues of concern.

First, there is too much inventory of some product lines in the warehouse. The value of this inventory is falling due to deterioration and developments in consumer electronics. The Sales and Production managers have been alerted to the need either to 'push' the slow-moving product lines harder to customers or to adjust production plans to produce fewer items.

Meanwhile, cash flow summaries have highlighted another problem. The Purchasing department accepts 30-day credit terms from suppliers, and insists that they be paid strictly on time. However, the Sales department is giving customers 60 days' credit, and is reluctant to press them for payment. Southfield Electronics is giving money out more readily than it is getting money in – reducing its working capital and creating a threat to its solvency, since its cash reserves are small. The Accounts Manager decides to call a meeting to discuss the need for longer credit terms with suppliers and stricter credit control with customers.

Activity 2: Email

As an accounts clerk at Southfield Electronics, you have been asked by the Chief Accountant to send a brief email to the Sales Manager, Hailey Skommett, notifying her of the cash flow situation, explaining its relevance to the Sales department. Today's date is 13 June 20X2.

Required
Complete the email using words from the picklist below.

EMAIL

To: hskommett@southfield.co.uk

From: yourname@southfield.co.uk

Date: 13/06/X2

Subject: Cash flow and credit control issues

I'm sure you know how important it is to maintain [▼] cash flow, so that the organisation has sufficient day to day funds to maintain its operations and pay its [▼]. Recently, however, Southfield has been paying out money to suppliers [▼] than it has been collecting money from customers. The Sales department obviously has a key role in this, through its credit control policies. The Chief Accountant is keen to review this issue with you and the [▼].

Kind regards

YN

Picklist:

faster
negative
payables
positive
Production Manager
Purchasing Manager
receivables
slower

Assessment focus point

Tasks relating to the finance role are likely to be text based, with the possible inclusion of diagrams, for example relating to the provision of information to other roles inside, or outside, the organisation. In this context they may require the identification of relationships.

A similar type of text-based task can also present a list of actions, requiring that actions appropriate to a situation are identified, for example aiding the solvency of an organisation.

Like all text-based tasks, the requirements and answers will need careful reading, identifying key words within statements such as 'not', or 'before' or 'after' a date.

You should also be prepared for scenarios within different types of organisations, noting that the typical retail organisation may have different functions compared to a manufacturing organisation, or a wholesale organisation. Similarly, service-based organisations like an accountancy practice will have different functions compared to a goods-based organisation.

6 The legal framework

Organisations operate within a framework of laws which is very broad in scope, and deals with a range of specific issues. While you don't have to know about specific legislation in detail for this unit, you are expected to appreciate the importance of an organisation's compliance with the law of the land or region in which it operates.

Compliance with all areas of the law is important because:

- The law is there to protect people from loss and suffering, and ensure minimum acceptable standards of management

- There may be financial penalties (eg fines, compensation) and operational penalties (eg loss of licence) for non-compliance

- Non-compliance can damage the reputation of the organisation, and its ability to attract investors, customers and staff

- Non-compliance can lead to burdens and costs of corrective action, closer scrutiny in future and so on

For an organisation in the UK, the main sources of law are UK statutes (or Acts of Parliament), EU Directives issued by the European Union, and regulations made under those laws.

It is the responsibility of every member of an organisation to comply with legislation (where you could reasonably be expected to be aware of provisions, as relevant to your job role) – and to monitor and ensure compliance within the area of your responsibility. For example, you have a personal duty not to discriminate against others; not to misuse personal data held on file; not to break health and safety rules;

not to engage in criminal activities such as theft or assault at work – and to take appropriate steps if you see anyone else doing so.

As a member of an accounting or payroll function, you also have a shared duty to support the organisation's compliance with requirements for financial controls, records and reports.

The following are some examples of areas regulated under UK and EU law – many of which will have their equivalents in the legal regimes of other parts of the world.

Area of the law	Examples
How the organisation does business	**Contract law:** what constitutes a valid contract, and how rights and obligations under a contract can be enforced **Data protection and confidentiality:** what personal data organisations can legitimately hold and use, to protect the privacy of individuals **Intellectual property:** protecting the rights of the originators of product designs, written texts and artistic works, by preventing their copying and exploitation by others
How the organisation treats its employees	**Employment protection:** protecting employees from unfair dismissal and redundancy practices **Health and safety:** protection of employees and visitors in the workplace **Working conditions, pay and benefits:** minimum standards for remuneration, working hours and so on **Diversity and equal opportunity:** protection against harassment and discrimination at work on the grounds of sex, sexual orientation, race, religion, age or disability
Responsibilities to shareholders/stakeholders (Company law and corporate governance)	Duties of directors of the company Keeping accounts and registers Preparing and auditing financial statements Preparing and circulating annual reports and accounts
Responsibilities to the State	Collection and payment of taxes including VAT to HM Revenue & Customs (HMRC) Compilation and provision of reports and returns

6.1 Regulatory control

In addition to legislation, there has been an increase in the guidance, monitoring and control of organisational practices through 'watchdog' bodies, voluntary Codes of Practice and industry standards.

- Regulatory bodies oversee the activities of businesses in various areas: examples include the Financial Reporting Council (FRC) and the Health and Safety Executive.

- Codes of Practice may be agreed by industry representative or advisory bodies. For example, there are standards covering the reporting of financial performance (International Financial Reporting Standards) and the verification of reports by auditors (International Standards on Auditing).

- Professional bodies (like the chartered accountancy bodies and the AAT) develop and enforce standards of competence, ethical conduct and continuing professional education in their members.

Chapter summary

- An organisation pursues a wide range of activities in pursuit of its objectives, and these activities are generally grouped as specialist 'functions'.

- Line functions (such as production and sales) directly further the primary activities of the business, while staff functions (such as accounting and finance) support them by providing resources, policies and information.

- The financial functions in an organisation include financial accounting, management accounting and payroll.

- Their main role is to support managers and staff in other functions by preparing and providing complete, accurate and timely information on the financial implications of their activities (including employing people).

- By providing this information, people in financial roles make an important contribution to the smooth running and efficiency of the business (by supporting planning, control and decision making); the solvency of the business (by managing working capital, highlighting the cash flow implications of activity, and providing information about debts and the availability of funds to cover them); and the legal compliance of the business (in areas such as financial controls, records and statements).

- Accounting and payroll staff are always required to follow the rules and procedures laid down by their organisation to ensure that legislative and regulatory requirements are complied with.

- Legal compliance embraces not just accounting and payroll practices but also the conduct of the organisation and its employees, in areas such as data protection, health and safety at work, employment protection, equal opportunities and corporate governance.

Keywords

- **Cash flow:** Amounts of cash flowing into and out of the organisation

- **Control:** Using information about activities that have taken place in order to hold managers accountable for those activities and to make decisions about how future activities should take place

- **Efficiency:** Achieving objectives with the minimum amount (and minimum waste) of resources

- **Financial accounting:** Activities mainly concerned with the processing and recording of transactions and the production of financial statements

- **Line functions:** Activities or departments, such as production and sales, which directly further organisational objectives

- **Management accounting:** Providing financial information to support management decision-making

- **Planning:** Using information about availability, costs and benefits of resources in order to make decisions about what will be done to achieve the organisation's objectives

- **Solvency:** The ability of the organisation to pay its debts when they fall due

- **Staff functions:** Activities or departments, such as accounting and finance, HR (personnel) and IT, which support line functions in their objectives

- **Stakeholders:** Individuals or other organisations who are affected by the activities of the organisation

- **Statutory financial statements:** Financial accounts used by external stakeholders and required by law; less detailed than management accounts

- **Working capital:** Day to day finance required for operational activities

Test your learning

1 **Which THREE of the following would be a staff function within an organisation?**

	✓
Human resources	
Manufacturing	
Stores control	
Accounting and finance	
Information technology	

2 **Match the elements of accounting (on the right) to either financial accounting or management accounting.**

Production of financial statements

Financial accounting

Prepares information for internal use

Processing and recording transactions

Management accounting

Prepares information for external use

Information for managers to make decisions

3 **Which of the following might be typical tasks involved in payroll?**

	✓
The calculation of gross pay	
Purchasing supplies	
The calculation of tax, National Insurance and other deductions	
Preparing payslips	
Bank reconciliations	
Paying cash into the bank	
Making up wages, or preparing data for direct credit (BACS)	

	✓
Writing cheques	
Distributing payslips to employees	

4 **Which TWO of the following are elements of efficiency?**

	✓
Providing a service at the least possible cost	
Minimum wastage	
Paying the minimum wage to employees	
Achieving objectives with minimum use of resources	

5 **Which TWO of the following laws, regulations or standards are likely to be most relevant to staff working in the Financial Accounts department of a UK retail business selling clothes in the UK?**

	✓
Health and safety regulation	
Pollution emission regulations	
HMRC VAT rules	
Regulations over the export of goods	

The organisational framework

2

Learning outcomes

1.2	Demonstrate an understanding of how finance staff contribute to an organisation's success
	• The different types of policies and procedures affecting finance staff: finance function-specific and organisation-wide.
1.4	Identify the importance of data security
	• Why it is important to ensure the security of data and information.
	• The implications to the organisation if data and information is not secure.
	• How data and information is retained securely: using passwords, archiving, backups and restricting access.

Assessment context

Policies and procedures, including data security, are an important part of the unit syllabus and are likely to be examined. This may be tested with scenarios or statements, after which relevant answers need to be selected.

Organisational structures and reporting lines represent important underpinning knowledge within the unit, but may not be directly examined.

Qualification context

Like the roles of finance staff, this topic is relevant to the start of the unit. Policies and procedures can be linked with other topics, such as communication skills, for example when needing to explain or query them.

Reference to the organisational framework, policies and procedures may be made occasionally in other units in Levels 3 and 4, but not examined specifically.

Business context

Understanding the organisational framework would usually be a part of induction to an organisation. It should give employees a sense of the support network, and their responsibilities, within an organisation, and so contribute to better productivity and efficiency.

Chapter overview

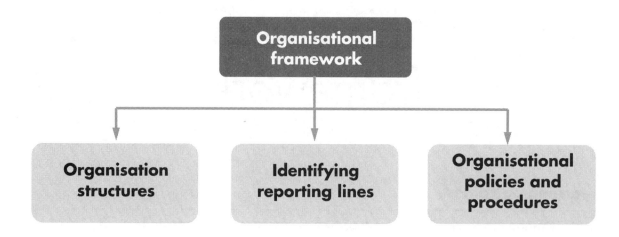

Introduction

This chapter looks at how the type of organisational structure can impact on the style of reporting in an organisation. We also cover how policies, and procedures can influence the working environment.

1 Organisation structure

Organisation structure is the 'shape' of an organisation, which reflects a number of decisions about how it will function most efficiently, including:

- How the organisation's tasks are grouped and divided to form different units, such as functions, departments and sections. This may be done on the basis of function (marketing, production, finance), geography (eg countries or sales territories) or product types.

- How power, authority and responsibility are allocated to different levels and positions in the organisation. This creates a hierarchy or **chain of command**, whereby authority flows 'down the line' from senior management to each level of the organisation – and accountability and reports flow back up.

- How different units, tiers and positions in the organisation are linked by lines of communication and co-operation – so that their plans and activities can be co-ordinated towards the achievement of overall objectives, and so that individuals and teams receive the information and resources they require to play their part.

1.1 Organisation charts

Organisation charts are often used to illustrate the formal structure of an organisation or function. In their most basic form, they use boxed or unboxed captions to indicate particular units (eg the accounting function) or positions (eg Accounts Manager) and linking lines to indicate the relationships and communication between them.

Vertical lines link different tiers or levels, illustrating chains of command (downwards) and reporting lines (upwards).

- Instructions, orders and work requests flow down the chain of command from people with more authority (superiors) to those with less authority (subordinates).

- Reports flow back up the line – because subordinates are **accountable** to superiors for the tasks they have been given. Queries may also flow back up the line, if subordinates need to seek or confirm instructions. Certain decisions may have to be 'referred' back up the line if subordinates lack the authority to handle them themselves.

- Your **line manager** is your immediate superior, following the vertical line of command: this is the person directly responsible for requesting work from you and to whom you report directly.

Horizontal lines link units/positions at the same level of the organisation, which are grouped together under the 'umbrella' of the next level up. Units/positions linked in this way need to communicate and co-ordinate their work to meet their shared objectives. They may occasionally be required to work together in **cross-functional teams** for projects requiring special co-ordination.

A horizontal line joining a vertical line from the side is often used to show 'staff' relationships, where a unit or position doesn't have direct authority 'over' the next tier down – but exercises influence by giving expert advice, or developing and enforcing policies or procedures, in relevant areas of work.

An IT department may exercise influence over other departments' IT systems development and data security procedures, say – while an Accounts department may impose policies for budgeting, invoicing, payment authorisations, expenses claims and so on.

Illustration 1: An organisation chart

The organisation chart for Southfield Electronics is as follows, showing how the finance function fits into the overall scheme of things at the firm.

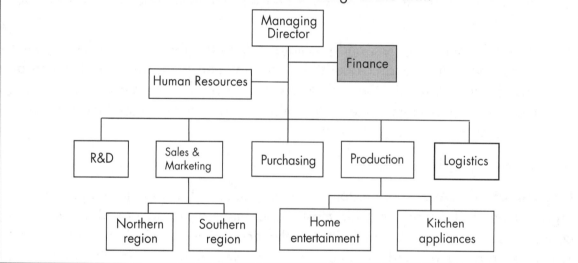

BPP
LEARNING MEDIA

The chart for the finance function is as follows.

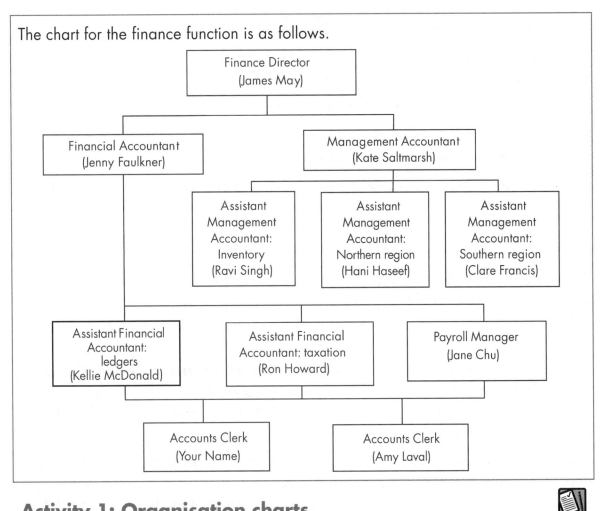

Activity 1: Organisation charts

Required

From the preceding organisation charts shown in Illustration 1 identify:

(a) How many people you (Accounts Clerk) directly report to

(b) Who you would ask if you don't know what to do with a memo about a staff member's National Insurance contributions

(c) Which three members of the Financial Accounts department have the same amount of authority

(d) What difficulties might be caused for you by these members having the same amount of authority

(e) Who you might appeal to if these difficulties were too much for you

(f) How a member of the R&D function should issue instructions to a member of the Kitchen Appliances production team

(g) Whether the finance function has 'line' or 'staff' authority to impose a credit control policy in the Logistics department

1.2 Document and information flows

The **organisation structure** affects the accounting system, and the role of the accounting and payroll functions, in terms of:

- How information is collected, and by whom

- How information is sent up and down the organisation chain, and across the boundaries between different functions

- How information should be processed and presented, to suit the needs of different users

2 Identifying reporting lines

When you work within an organisation you are not working in isolation. As we have just seen, you may have colleagues or peers at the same level, managers of varying levels of seniority, and possibly more junior employees to whom you can delegate tasks.

Your job or role description often sets out the **reporting procedure** for that role. For whom are you doing tasks? Who needs particular data or documents next? To whom are you accountable for performing a task correctly? To whom should you refer questions and problems?

Reporting lines and procedures will differ from organisation to organisation, depending on the formal structure of the business. In a very small business, for example, all employees may report directly to the owner of the business. In a large multinational company, there could be complex organisational structures for the business as a whole, and each country, site or department within it.

2.1 Identifying reporting lines for a given job and task

You are most likely to report on a day to day basis to a designated supervisor or line manager such as the head of your department or section. A line manager is someone who has direct authority over people and activities, down the vertical 'line' of command in the organisation chart. In an Accounts department, this is likely to be an accountant or financial controller, or it could be the general office or administration manager.

If you are temporarily working on a particular project, you may report to the **project manager** on tasks relating to that specific project. An example might be if you were preparing costings for a new product launch, say, or checking supplier invoices for the installation of a new IT system: such activities may well be organised as a distinct project, with a designated project manager overseeing the work.

You may also find that, on occasion, you are required to do a one-off job for someone to whom you do not normally report. For example, the sales manager may have requested a breakdown of sales by geographical area: in this case, you may report directly to the sales manager on this specific task (by agreement with your line manager).

Organisational policies and procedures may suggest other reporting lines. For example, if you identify a health or safety risk in your workplace, the 'appropriate person' to report it to may be the Health and Safety Officer or Fire Officer.

It is important for you to know to whom you should report both on routine and non-routine matters. For routine tasks, this will most often be your immediate superior, project manager or the person who has asked you to perform a task.

In cases where a matter has to be referred 'above the head' of your immediate superior(s) for a decision, you should simply follow the vertical line of command up to the next highest person. An example might be where you cannot resolve a conflict with an immediate superior: if they have asked you to do something inappropriate or unethical, say, or have treated you unfairly.

Illustration 2: Identifying reporting lines

At Southfield Electronics, there are two accounts clerks – yourself and Amy Laval – employed as a 'shared resource' for two assistant financial accountants and a payroll manager.

Your role includes fulfilling work requests given to you by all three of these individuals, and giving clerical support, as required, to the work of the financial accounts section as a whole.

One day:

- You are struggling to complete a piece of work given to you by Ron Howard, which appears to contain incomplete information.

- You have just finished a batch of payslips, which need checking.

- You have just received a delivery of stationery supplies for the section but, before signing the receipt note, you notice that the delivery does not seem to be complete, according to the copy of the purchase order sent to you by the Purchasing department.

- Both Kellie McDonald and Ron Howard have given you urgent tasks to perform the following day, and you know you will not have time to do both of them. You have spoken to both Kellie and Ron about this – but neither of them will back down: they each think their work is most important.

What are the appropriate reporting and referral lines in this situation?

- Your queries about the first task should be referred to Ron Howard, because he was the one who gave you the task.

- The payslips should be given to Jane Chu (the Payroll Manager) for checking, because this is the work area for which she is responsible.

- The query about the stationery order should be referred to the Purchasing department, since they are responsible for the purchase order, and dealing with suppliers.

- If Kellie and Ron cannot come to agreement, you may have to refer the matter to their superior, who has the authority to decide whose work has priority.

---

3 Organisational policies and procedures

Organisational policies and procedures will influence most aspects of your everyday working practice, both in technical matters (ie how accounting and information-processing tasks should be carried out) and in regard to your behaviour in the workplace (including areas such as health, safety and security, timekeeping, dress, **confidentiality** of information, and recycling and other 'green' practices).

> **Confidentiality** is the duty not to disclose restricted, private or otherwise sensitive information to unauthorised parties.

Key term

A **policy** is a statement of how an organisation wants and expects activities to be carried out. They provide strong guidelines for action, decision making and problem solving. Equal opportunities policies, for example, are statements of the organisation's attitude to eliminating discrimination in the workplace, and how this should be done in selecting people for jobs, training, rewards and promotions.

A **procedure** is a standard sequence of steps or operations necessary to perform an activity. An organisation will have formal or informal procedures relating to a wide range of matters, such as the handling of cash receipts, the recording of payroll details, the processing of expenses claims, the authorisation of payments and the secure storage of data.

3.1 Why is it important to adhere to policy and procedure?

Often, policies and procedures are regarded as routine – or even as a nuisance, if there are more convenient 'short cuts' in performing a task. However, it is important to adhere to formal organisation requirements – and to know why you are doing so.

Policies and procedures are put in place to:

- **Support efficiency**. They enable people to perform routine, repetitive or foreseeable tasks correctly, without having to waste time and resources analysing and planning them afresh every time: in other words, you don't have to 'reinvent the wheel'.

- **Support compliance**. They generally build in the requirements of law and regulation, ensuring minimum standards of practice (and possibly 'good' practice).

- **Protect people**. Health, safety and security policies and procedures, for example, are put in place to protect you, others working around you and people visiting your workplace.

- **Protect finance, property, information and other assets of the organisation**. Financial control procedures, for example, are established to minimise temptations and opportunities for fraud and mismanagement of resources.

Procedures may also incorporate rules. If a policy is 'the way it should be done', and a procedure is 'the way it is done', a rule is 'the way it must be done (in order to be done correctly)'. Examples of rules include maintaining the confidentiality of financial information, seeking required authorisations for transactions, and keeping fire doors clear and closed.

Let's look briefly at some of the organisational policies and procedures that are most likely to affect your work in an accounting or payroll environment.

3.2 Health and safety

Most policies and procedures for health and safety in the workplace are based on provisions set out in law such as the Health and Safety at Work Act 1974 and related regulations.

Health and safety at work is about the prevention of accidents and ill-health caused by working conditions and work practices.

All organisations with five or more employees must have a written Health and Safety Policy, continually updated and circulated to all employees. As an employee, you have a duty to study this document: you will normally be asked to sign a form stating that you have read it and are willing to take responsibility (in relevant areas) for complying with the policy.

Specific occupational health and safety policies may cover a range of issues such as:

- The duty of all employees and managers to contribute to a healthy and safe work environment
- The use of safety measures and equipment, where required
- Non-smoking
- The participation of staff in regular fire and evacuation drills
- The reporting of risks and accidents to appropriate officials (eg a health and safety or fire officer)

There should be detailed procedures for operations such as:

- The use of fire alarms and equipment
- The evacuation of the premises in the event of fire or other threats
- The labelling, storage and handling of potentially dangerous workplace chemicals
- The safe use and maintenance of electrical equipment and dangerous tools
- The reporting of identified health and safety hazards
- The recording of accidents (eg in an accident book)

Illustration 3: Evacuation procedure

Southfield Electronics has a range of policies and procedures, which are published in procedure manuals for each function and work site, and also posted on the corporate intranet for employees to consult on their computer terminals.

Its Evacuation Procedure, for example, appears as follows.

EVACUATION OF THE PREMISES IN THE EVENT OF EMERGENCY

In the event of an emergency such as fire or terrorist threat all employees are required to leave the building by the designated route as quickly as possible. They are advised to remain calm and not to linger to gather personal belongings.

Employees are advised not to use the lifts in the event of a fire emergency, as lifts may cease to operate at any time. Particular attention should be paid to evacuees who have special needs (for example, those in wheelchairs or with impaired sight or hearing), and members of staff should help them out.

Once they have left the building, employees and visitors should go immediately to the designated Assembly Point and ensure that any visitors or others on the premises at the time of evacuation, who do not know where to go, are directed and assisted to the Assembly Point by members of staff.

Employees should wait at the Assembly Point. The Safety Officer will carry a roster of everyone signed in as being in the building, and will 'call a roll' at the Assembly Point. Each person should respond when their name is called.

No one is permitted to return to the building until instructed to do so by a senior official or the Safety Officer.

Activity 2: Evacuation procedure

You are the Accounts Clerk at Southfield Electronics, and you have noticed that several members of the Accounts department have been taking the lifts, or even staying in the offices, during fire evacuation drills. You have a word with your supervisor about this, and she refers you to the Safety Officer.

Required

(a) **For each action provided, select whether they are correct or incorrect actions to carry out during a drill (according to the evacuation procedure).**

Action	Correct/Incorrect
Leave the building by the designated route as quickly (but calmly) as possible, not lingering to gather personal belongings	▼
Use lifts in the event of a fire emergency	▼
Go immediately to the designated Assembly Point and ensure that any visitors are directed and assisted	▼
Pay particular attention to people with special needs (eg those in wheelchairs or with impaired sight or hearing)	▼
Stay quiet when your name is called by the Safety Officer who will 'call a roll' of everyone signed in as being in the building	▼
Do not return to the building until instructed to do so by a senior official or the Safety Officer	▼

Picklist:

Correct
Incorrect

(b) **Explain the importance of complying with the procedure during drills.**

3.3 Security

Security policies and procedures are designed to protect the physical security of assets (such as computers and petty cash); the physical security of employees (eg from attack or intimidation); and the security of information (eg from unauthorised access, theft or tampering).

Security measures in an office environment can range from simple rules about locking doors, windows, filing cabinets and petty cash boxes at the end of the day to more complex procedures for:

- Controlling access to areas of a building (eg using security doors, sign-in procedures and identity badges or security cards)

- Controlling access to the computer system (eg using passwords and authorisation codes)

- Training staff to handle potentially unsafe situations, and to report unidentified strangers and intruders in the office

3.4 Working hours and timekeeping

Policies will generally be laid out in regard to issues such as:

- Working hours
- Office opening hours
- The taking of lunch breaks (and holiday entitlements)
- Timekeeping and punctuality

There may be detailed procedures for clocking on and off, filling out timesheets, operating flexi-time schemes and other forms of flexible working – and so on.

Such issues are important for:

- The efficiency of the organisation, ensuring that it can plan for adequate staffing – and rely on those plans, once made

- Fraud prevention, ensuring that people work the hours they are paid for

- Effective working relations, ensuring people honour their commitments to the team and 'pull their weight'

- Individual wellbeing, ensuring some 'work–life balance' – which also supports long-term productivity

- Individual work planning and scheduling, ensuring that workloads are planned within the hours available in the day! (We look at this in more detail later in the Course Book.)

3.5 Maintenance of your work area

Your personal **work area** may include your desk, the area around your desk, and other areas of the office in which you regularly move and work.

Your immediate work area will often be your own responsibility, in general terms. It will, to some degree, define you to your colleagues – and external visitors. If your desk is tidy and documents are filed away, this gives an impression of a tidy mind and an efficient employee. Conversely, an untidy work area may create the impression of someone who does not care about their work. A tidy and organised work area also ensures that you – and others around you – can work effectively and efficiently: we look at this further later in the Course Book.

There may be departmental rules or guidelines as to how your work area should be organised and maintained, mainly aimed at ensuring that offices maintain a professional image, and reflect the corporate image of the organisation, particularly in areas which are visited by outsiders.

Organisations often have rules regarding personal effects displayed in work areas, such as photographs of family and friends, posters or postcards. This will often depend upon the type of environment in which you work. In a large open plan office which rarely receives visits from external parties such as customers, suppliers or the general public, it might be quite acceptable to have family photographs or amusing cartoons displayed (providing that they do not offend those working around you).

However, in an office regularly visited by customers, the desire to convey professionalism may lead to organisational restrictions on the type or number of personal possessions allowed in the workplace.

Even if there are no formal 'rules' regarding such matters, there may be informal 'understandings'. Ask colleagues or your supervisor, or observe the work areas of your colleagues to find out what is appropriate.

Another important aspect of this is that tidiness supports data security. You will generally be expected to tidy away confidential documents once they are finished with, or likely to be left unattended. However, in some organisations, there may be an explicit **clear desk policy**, which requires that everything must be cleared from your desktop at the end of each day, in order to ensure disciplined work practices and to reduce the vulnerability of data to theft and espionage.

3.6 Confidentiality of information

In an accounting role, you will come across a variety of confidential information – and you must be extremely careful how you deal with it. As we saw earlier in this chapter, you have a key role in co-ordinating flows of financial information in the organisation. But what information should 'flow' – and to whom? What is 'confidential' information?

Some information (in files, reports, emails or letters, say) may be clearly marked as being 'confidential' (or 'private', 'limited access' or 'for authorised individuals only').

Certain types of information may be designated as confidential by law, regulation, organisational policy and professional Codes of Practice.

- Details of customers and suppliers must not be disclosed to anyone outside the organisation.

- Personal data about employees, for example payroll details, must be kept strictly confidential, to protect privacy.

- Organisations that process personal information need to comply with the EU General Data Protection Regulation (GDPR), and also the UK Data Protection Act. The aim of both of these regulations is to protect information, and data that organisations hold on individuals. This includes security, privacy, and how the information is used.

- Financial information is likely to be highly sensitive – but there are other categories of information which, if disclosed, could be used for purposes harmful to the organisation or its personnel: there are likely to be strict rules about the disclosure of security procedures and codes, details of legal proceedings, new product plans and so on.

Illustration 4: Confidentiality issue

At Southfield Electricals, the sales manager has forwarded to the Financial Accountant a letter from an estate agent, requesting financial information about one of the firm's major customers, which is applying to rent a commercial property. The information is needed as soon as possible, by fax or email, in order to secure approval for the rental. The Sales Manager has asked the Accounts department to help.

Is there a confidentiality issue here? Yes, there is. The Financial Accountant would certainly need the customer's permission to disclose any information. Since the request seems inappropriate, she should also confirm the identity of the person making the request. If everything is above board, there is still a confidentiality issue in how the information is sent: fax can be easily intercepted (and so can email). The information should be sent securely, and clearly marked 'private and confidential'.

Activity 3: Providing information

You have been asked for the following information. Should each item be provided?

Required

Indicate whether you would provide the information or, if not, indicate the reason why.

	Yes – provide information	No – personal information	No – confidential information
A customer asks for the address and telephone number of another customer	☐	☐	☐
A colleague asks you for the home address of two other employees	☐	☐	☐
The company's security guard asks for the names of the visitors expected by your department that week	☐	☐	☐

3.7 Secure storage of data and information

Information held in files, records and computers needs to be protected from accidental or malicious damage, loss, theft, sabotage, interference – and prying eyes. Interference may just be casual – someone playing around with your terminal when you are not there – but it can still result in damage, disruption or loss of data. Potential threats to data security include computer viruses, hacking or 'phishing', systems failure and corruption/loss of data.

It is especially important to keep accounting data secure, because it is needed to run the business properly; it is often commercially sensitive; and (as in the case of personnel and payroll data) it may be private, confidential and protected by privacy and data protection laws.

There will almost certainly be policies and procedures covering data security aspects such as:

- The non-removal of data and equipment from the premises

- The frequent backing-up of computerised data, and the storage of backups separately from the original data, so that there are safe copies in case of systems failure, data corruption or fire

- The use of anti-virus software, firewalls and other protective tools on all computers, to prevent malicious corruption and theft of data

- The use of passwords to prevent unauthorised users from gaining access to computer systems or files (often with additional policies regarding the complexity and regular change of passwords)

- The use of authorisations to control access to security-coded paper-based files

- The non-divulging of passwords, security codes and other data security measures to other parties

3.8 Document retention

There will be additional policies and procedures for document retention: the period that documents need to be kept on file. There are legal obligations to keep certain financial documents for prescribed lengths of time.

- Many accounting and banking records (including ledgers, invoices, cheques, paying-in counterfoils, bank statements and instructions to banks) should be kept for six years.

- Employee records (including staff personnel records, time cards and piecework records, payroll records and expenses claims) should also be kept for six years – and accident report books, permanently!

If in doubt, you should consult organisational policy documents, or your supervisor, to check what the policies and procedures are – and look out for any specific policy information set out in the assessment.

3.9 Departmental deadlines

Some activities of financial functions are bound by strict deadlines, and these should be clearly incorporated in relevant plans and procedures.

Payroll preparation is one example. If an employee is to be paid on the 30th of the month, the pay must be in their bank account on that date. Any changes to pay rates must be included on the first available payroll. Tax deductions have to be paid over to HM Revenue & Customs by a due date: if payment is delayed, the employer may have to pay interest. Similarly, other deductions, such as pension contributions, need to be paid over to third parties regularly and on time, otherwise the employee's entitlements could be affected.

In financial accounting, there are strict, externally imposed deadlines for the preparation and lodging of statutory financial statements and reports (eg the year-end lodgement date). These, in turn, impose internal deadlines for the gathering and processing of information, auditing and so on.

However, as we will see in later chapters, it is very important to meet any agreed departmental or team deadline for the completion of work, because your work impacts on the work of others.

Illustration 5: Keeping to deadlines

One of your tasks at Southfield Electronics is to list any cheques received in the post each morning. This listing is then passed on to the cashier, James Thorne, for entry into the cash receipts book and updating of the receivables ledger (sales ledger). He can only carry out his daily task once you have finished yours.

If you do not finish the cheque listing early in the morning (because you have not planned your work routine) or if you mislay the cheque listing for the day (because your work area is untidy or your files disordered), this will impact on James's work for the day as well as yours.

3.10 Authorisation procedures

Many accounting and payroll tasks require authorisations, as part of the organisation's system of financial controls to prevent fraud and mismanagement of resources. An authorisation is a point in a procedure at which confirmation or permission to proceed must be obtained from an individual with appropriate authority.

In payroll, for example:

- All variations to the payroll must be properly authorised, including temporary variations such as overtime. Permanent variations, such as salary increases, will usually be authorised by senior managers and it is likely that you will be familiar with their signatures. However, overtime is likely to be authorised by line managers. The employee's record or contract of employment will let you know if they are entitled to overtime payments – but how do you know if the actual overtime figure has been correctly authorised?

- Most large organisations will have a list of **authorised signatories** for each department. This is a list of people authorised to approve changes to the payroll, together with a specimen signature. The list should also indicate whether the person can authorise permanent and/or temporary changes, to what value, for what department, and to what grades of employee. If you are a payroll clerk, you will need a copy of this list so that you can check that variations are correctly authorised!

- If variations are not correctly authorised, you will need to bring this to your supervisor's or line manager's attention. (Do not assume that it is an innocent mistake: the employee could be trying to obtain an increased salary or overtime payments fraudulently...)

Similar policies and procedures (involving authorisations and designated signatories) will invariably be in place for operations such as:

- The issuing of purchase orders
- The preparation of cheques and other payments
- The processing of expense claims
- The processing of petty cash

These policies may vary from organisation to organisation, but the principles will be similar.

Activity 4: Authorisation

Required

What information will you need to know, and check, to ensure that authorisations comply with procedure?

You should be informed of the specific policies and procedures applicable to your work role, via policy documents and procedure manuals (and their online equivalents) and/or by induction, training and coaching within your department.

The most important point is that individuals working in financial roles need to:

- Find out what the applicable policies and procedures are
- Ensure that they understand the requirements (or seek help to understand them)
- Ensure that they follow or adhere to the requirements, in all relevant situations

Illustration 6: Payment authorisation

Southfield Electronics has a policy about authorising expenditure.

Ian Hamilton, an employee in the Sales department, has been asked to organise the office Christmas party. He has booked caterers for the event, but they require a deposit of £150.

Ian must fill in a cheque requisition form, giving details of the payment, and attach a VAT invoice or receipt as evidence of the payment. Ian doesn't have such documentation, so just puts 'None' in the space on the cheque requisition form.

The form is sent to the Sales Supervisor for authorisation. However, she knows that for amounts between £100 and £500, requisitions must be authorised by a department manager. The form is therefore forwarded to the Sales Manager – who signs it, and sends it to the Financial Accounts department.

Jenny Faulkner calls the Sales Manager to point out that the requisition should not have been authorised, and cannot be processed, in the absence of evidence of payment. The requisition form will be returned to Ian. Jenny advises that Ian, or the Sales Manager, can pay the deposit himself – and then fill out a cheque requisition for reimbursement, attaching the VAT receipt for the expense. However, they will have to bear in mind that correctly completed and authorised cheque requisition forms must be with the Accounts department by 10am to guarantee that a cheque is prepared on the same day.

Meanwhile, the company also has a written agreement with its bank regarding who is allowed to sign the organisation's cheques. The bank will only accept cheques that have been signed by the authorised signatories. For cheques up to a value of £8,000, the signature of a director is required. Cheques for more than this amount require the signatures of two directors.

Assessment focus point

Assessment tasks for this topic are likely to be short text-based questions where you may be asked to select relevant policies and procedures, or true statements. As with many text-based questions, marks are more likely to be gained by careful reading of the whole task before committing answers.

Chapter summary

- Organisation structure reflects the grouping of tasks into units and functions; the flow of authority and responsibility; and lines of communication and co-operation between individuals and units. This can be depicted in organisation charts.

- The organisation structure partly determines reporting lines, in establishing a 'chain of command'. Your designated supervisor or line manager is your direct superior in this chain, to whom you report most directly.

- Reporting lines and relationships are also based on who asked you to perform a given task; who is the manager of the project to which the task contributes; and who is the most appropriate person to deal with a given matter. Some matters may need to be 'referred upwards' to a superior manager.

- Organisational policies and procedures will influence most aspects of your everyday working practice. It is important to adhere to them, to support efficiency and compliance – and to protect people and assets.

- Some key examples of policies and procedures in an accounting environment include health and safety; security; working hours and timekeeping; maintenance of your work area; confidentiality of information; secure storage of data and information; document retention; adherence to departmental deadlines; and authorisations and designated signatories.

Keywords

- **Accountable:** The duty of a subordinate to report to a superior on the outcome of the tasks they have been given

- **Authorised signatories:** People who are authorised to sign the organisation's cheques and to authorise other operations

- **Chain of command:** The line down which authority flows in the organisation structure

- **Clear desk policy:** An organisational policy that all desks must be left clear at the end of each working day

- **Confidentiality:** The duty not to disclose restricted, private or otherwise sensitive information to unauthorised parties

- **Cross-functional teams:** Teams which include members from different functions in the organisation, for the purpose of co-ordination (eg in carrying out projects)

- **Line manager:** Your immediate superior in the line or chain of command

- **Organisation charts:** Diagrams depicting the formal structure of an organisation

- **Organisation structure:** The 'shape' of an organisation, made up of defined units, levels of authority and communication lines

- **Policy:** A statement of how an organisation wants and expects activities to be carried out

- **Procedure:** A standard sequence of steps necessary to perform an activity

- **Project manager:** The manager appointed to run a particular project

- **Reporting procedure:** The channels through which an employee reports to a superior official

- **Work area:** Your desk, chair, surrounding furniture and space

Test your learning

1 Given below are examples of types of information that flow either down or up the organisation structure. **Tick the appropriate boxes to decide whether this is a downward flow or an upward flow.**

	Downward ✓	Upward ✓
Instructions	☐	☐
Exception reports	☐	☐
Briefings	☐	☐
Queries and questions	☐	☐
Plans	☐	☐
Routine reports	☐	☐
Decisions	☐	☐

2 You have been asked to prepare a 'To Do list' for the Accounts department, in relation to the relocation of the company's offices. This is being managed as a cross-functional project by the Office Manager. Because of the pressure of work from the Accounts Supervisor, you are not sure you will be able to complete the To Do list in the time given to you. **Who should you report to about this?**

Picklist:

Accounts Supervisor
Office Manager

3 Most employees like to personalise their work area with personal objects. **In which of the following work areas would this be most acceptable?**

▼

Picklist:

Accounts department where there are rarely any visits from non-employees
Reception area which is open to the public
Sales department where regular meetings are held with customers

4   Would you supply the following information? Enter Y for yes, N for No.

Your supervisor asks you for details of the latest R&D expenditure on new products.

A telephone caller, saying she is a financial journalist, asks you for details of your upcoming plans for new products.

A customer calls asking for the bank details of one of your fellow employees, stating that the customer wishes to pay a cheque into her bank account.

One of the senior accounts assistants has asked you to photocopy the notes for a training course that another rival company uses. You notice that the course notes have the copyright © symbol on them.

5   Complete the following sentences.

[▼] are points in a procedure at which confirmation or permission to proceed must be obtained from an individual with appropriate authority.

[▼] are people who are authorised to sign documents (eg for authorisation purposes) or company cheques.

Picklist:

Accountants
Authorisations
Designated signatories
Managers
Policies
Requests

Personal skills

3

Learning outcomes

2.1	**Identify the interpersonal skills required by finance staff**
	• A range of interpersonal skills: respecting others, developing trust, being responsible, being reliable, communicating effectively, negotiation, problem solving, decision making
	• How to use active listening skills
	• How to use appropriate business language
	• The importance of appropriate language, personal appearance and body language in different business situations to project a professional image
	• How interpersonal skills help build good business relationships
3.1	**Produce accurate work in appropriate formats**
	• Produce accurate information, which is technically correct and free from spelling and grammatical errors
	• Use numerical functions for business calculations in any combination: addition, subtraction, multiplication, division, percentages, proportions, ratios, averages and fractions
3.2	**Communicate information effectively**
	• Communicate using acceptable business language
	• Produce written communication that is clear, structured and follows a logical progression
	• Prepare logical and clearly structured notes to plan for verbal communications

Assessment context

Personal skills, including communication, literacy and numeracy skills, are an important part of the unit syllabus, and are likely to be examined. The assessment may test knowledge and skills required to communicate effectively in a range of formats and contexts. This will focus on communicating clearly, using business language, and demonstrating numeracy skills appropriate to your role. Personal qualities such as respect, trust, responsibility and reliability will also be addressed.

Qualification context

The themes of this chapter will reoccur and be developed in the following chapters on 'Presenting information' (reports, letters, emails), 'Working independently' and 'Working as part of a team'. They will also be relevant when considering the chapter 'Developing skills and knowledge'.

References to these themes, and techniques such as numerical calculations, may be used occasionally in other units in Levels 3 and 4, but not examined specifically.

Business context

Personal skills are a vital ingredient of success in management and business. They enable employees to communicate effectively with their colleagues, clients and customers, both as individuals and in groups, thus improving business performance.

Chapter overview

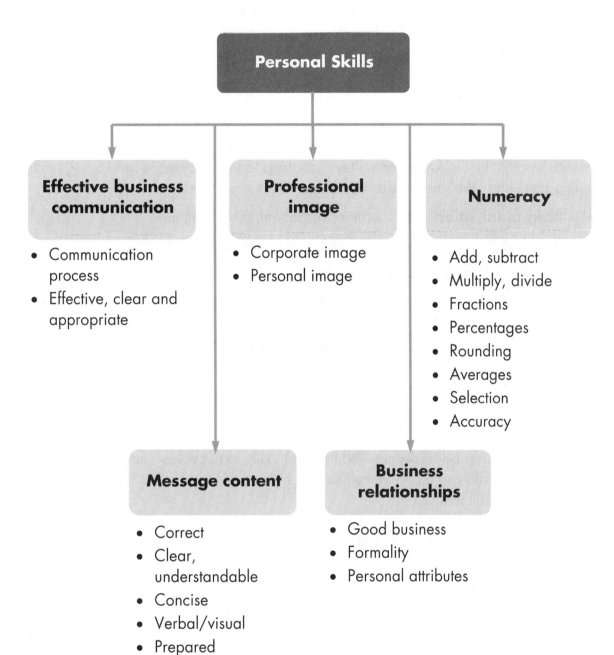

Personal Skills

Effective business communication

- Communication process
- Effective, clear and appropriate

Professional image

- Corporate image
- Personal image

Numeracy

- Add, subtract
- Multiply, divide
- Fractions
- Percentages
- Rounding
- Averages
- Selection
- Accuracy

Message content

- Correct
- Clear, understandable
- Concise
- Verbal/visual
- Prepared

Business relationships

- Good business
- Formality
- Personal attributes

Introduction

This chapter covers important skills that are required to be an effective employee in the workplace. These skills can include communication, and numeracy skills, along with good interpersonal skills.

1 Personal skills

These are skills concerned with how people manage and express themselves. Developing your personal skills can improve your success both socially and professionally. In the workplace they can help an employee to get along with colleagues, and other business relationships. Examples include:

- **Communication** skills – written, verbal and other methods

- Listening skills – receiving information accurately and completely

- Image – appearance and body language

- Personal qualities – respect, trust, responsibility, reliability, co-operation, initiative, creativity, problem solving, and many others

Many of these are often also called **'interpersonal skills'**, a phrase that refers to attributes that one human may use to interact with others. Being co-operative plainly involves another person, while being reliable is a stand-alone attribute.

Another phrase covering all the above, sometimes used in job descriptions, is 'soft skills'. In contrast, 'hard skills' refer to a person's knowledge and technical skills, which may include bookkeeping. While hard skills may be learned and perfected over time, soft skills are more difficult to acquire and change, but many courses and resources are available.

2 Effective business communication

2.1 What is business communication?

As we saw earlier, work effectively in finance is fundamentally about the effective preparation, giving and receiving of information. As we will see in later chapters, it is also about work effectively with other people to achieve shared objectives. All of this means: communication!

Communication is, at its most basic, the transmission or exchange of information: putting across a message. However, there are many different purposes for doing this:

- To inform: to give people data they require

- To persuade: to get others to agree to, or do, something

- To request: to ask for something

- To confirm: to check that data is correct and that different parties have the same understanding of it

- To build effective working relationships

All of these activities underpin efficient working and constructive working relationships.

2.2 The communication process

Effective communication is a two-way process, often shown as a 'cycle'. Signals or messages are sent by the communicator and received by the target recipient, who sends back some form of confirmation that the message has been received and understood.

Some means of communication are more appropriate and effective than others in different business contexts. If you get the choice of whether to carry out a communication task using a letter, memo, email, report or informal note – or, in real working life, a telephone call or face to face discussion – you will need to consider factors such as whether speed is important; whether there is the need for written confirmation; which format will best support you in getting your message across to the recipient; and which is the most efficient method in terms of time and cost. This is considered in more detail in Chapter 5.

Activity 1: Communication mediums

Required

Suggest the most effective medium for communication in the following situations using the drop down list.

Situation	Medium
New stationery is urgently required from the office goods supplier.	▼
The Managing Director wants to give a message to all staff.	▼
A member of staff has been absent five times in the past month, and her manager intends to take action.	▼
You need information quickly from another department.	▼
You have to explain a complicated procedure to a group of people.	▼

Picklist:

Face to face conversation
Meeting
Notice board/intranet
Telephone

2.3 Communicating effectively, clearly and appropriately

This unit requires you to demonstrate that you can 'communicate effectively, clearly and appropriately' in a range of work-related tasks. So what makes communication effective, clear and appropriate?

Attribute	Explanation
Using appropriate formats	Selecting the right format (letter, email, memorandum etc) for the job
Observing format conventions and house style	Using formats correctly: observing conventions of structure, format and style, within organisational guidelines and 'house style'
Professionally presented	Ensuring that documents are neat, legible, concise, helpfully structured and smartly presented: showing competence and awareness of business needs
Technically correct	Ensuring that content is accurate, appropriately detailed (for different levels of requirement) and checked for factual/data and typographical errors
Clearly understandable	Tailored to the writer's purpose in communicating (so that a clear message is sent) and to the information needs, language and capabilities of its audience (so that the message can be received)
Projecting the appropriate corporate image	Reflecting a general image of professionalism and competence – including appropriate formality – and the specific desired image or 'character' of the organisation
Achieving its purpose	Obtain feedback to check that the communication has been **effective**. Has it 'done its job'? Has it got the response it aimed for? If not: adjust and try again!

3 Message content

3.1 Technically correct

The information you provide, in an accounting role, is likely to be relied on by others, and factual and numerical errors may have serious consequences for their decision making and results – and for your performance evaluation, credibility and reputation!

This should go without saying, and it is perhaps unlikely that you would knowingly give out information that is technically incorrect. However, there is always the possibility of unknowingly conveying inaccurate information, or making careless errors – and you should be aware of this at all times.

- You may need to verify information, by checking the accuracy of the source, or cross-checking with other sources.

- If you are not confident in your knowledge or competence in a particular area, you may need to check with a more expert colleague, or with your supervisor.

- Always check the assumptions, logical processes and numerical operations (or 'workings') behind a piece of work, before submitting it.

3.2 Clear and understandable

It is always the responsibility of the sender of a message to ensure that the message has been received and understood: don't expect your target audience to do your work for you!

Take care with the language and terminology you use: tailor it to the needs and abilities of the person with whom you are communicating. In some cases you will be giving information to others in the Accounting department who are, like you, familiar with accounting terminology. However, if you are giving information to customers, or to the Marketing department, say, you could not take for granted that your accountancy knowledge will be shared!

Avoid **jargon**: technical terms or buzz words that only fellow technicians will know. Think about whether any diagrams you use will be meaningful to another person – and add labels and explanatory notes if you think a reader will need help 'decoding' your meaning.

When planning communications, think about your:

- **Purpose**: what do you need to get across? How do you need the other person to respond?

- **Audience**: what language will they understand? What are their needs?

- **Structure and Style**: what format, order, layout and language will be most helpful in achieving your purpose, given your intended audience?

(You might like to remember this as a checklist for message planning, with the helpful mnemonic: PASS!)

Illustration 1: Email message

Clare Francis is one of the assistant management accountants at Southfield Electronics. She has received a request from Kate Saltmarsh (the Management Accountant) and Taylor Smith (a new sales manager) for a summary of the comparison of the monthly sales per product type to budget for November. Both Kate and Taylor have requested the information to be sent via email.

Although Clare is sending the same information to both people, she decides to word the messages slightly differently. Kate is an accountant with detailed knowledge of accounting terminology, whereas it is unlikely that the new sales manager would have such detailed knowledge of the subject. The two emails might look like this.

EMAIL

To: ksaltmarsh@southfield.co.uk

From: cfrancis@southfield.co.uk

Date: 8 December 20X8

Subject: Sales variances – November

In response to your query, the following sales variances by product type were incurred in November:

Product	Variance
MP3 players	£14,300 adverse
Portable DVD players	£2,700 favourable
DVD/VHS combo players	£21,600 adverse
Digital TVs	£18,600 favourable

If you require further detail, let me know.

Clare

EMAIL

To: tsmith@southfield.co.uk

From: cfrancis@southfield.co.uk

Date: 8 December 20X8

Subject: Comparison of actual sales to budgeted sales – November

In response to your query, I have compared the **actual** sales per product type for November to the **budgeted** sales for that product, with the following results:

MP3 players	– sales were £14,300 less than budget
Portable DVD players	– sales were £2,700 more than budget
DVD/VHS combo players	– sales were £21,600 less than budget
Digital TVs	– sales were £18,600 more than budget

Clare

3.3 Keep it short and simple!

Here's another helpful mnemonic: KISS! Businesspeople have limited time in which to peruse communications – and that time is worth money to them and their organisations. So business communication, while never being abrupt or discourteous, should always be short, to the point, and easy to use. 'Keeping it Short and Simple' may mean:

- Ensuring your message is well structured (eg in clear topic paragraphs)

- Making it easy to read (eg legible and well spaced on the page, and written in reasonably short sentences)

- Being unambiguous (without potential misunderstandings from double-meaning words or vague phrases)

- Avoiding the use of jargon

- Eliminating unnecessary words and phrases

- Separating out detailed data, which would interrupt the flow of your main information or argument; detail can be placed in appendices or attachments, or summarised in tables or diagrams

3.4 Verbal or visual?

Consider what format will make your information clear, easy to use, professional-looking – and, if you are trying to be persuasive, impactful.

Verbal communication (using words or text) is useful for conveying the thread of an argument, and the meaning of information. However, it can overload readers with limited time to read and absorb. You might like to use visual elements – such as headings and bullet points – to organise textual information into more manageable 'chunks', with clear signposts for the reader.

Detailed data may be more clearly organised in a table, or headed columns, to show the reader how it is grouped and classified. Even more visual formats, such as charts, graphs and diagrams, may be used to highlight aspects such as comparisons, correlations and trends. (We look at the use of diagrams in Chapter 5, when we discuss report writing.)

3.5 Message preparation

When a meeting is prearranged (such as your staff appraisal, a team meeting, making a phone call), depending on the importance, it can be useful to prepare notes for verbal communication. This will help to organise your thoughts, ensure that you do not miss anything important, give you the opportunity to check facts, and consider appropriate language. Rough notes for your own use may also serve as a cue sheet during a meeting.

A suggested framework may be as follows.

- Your objectives
- Factual statements
- Problems highlighted
- Potential solutions

Similar notes could also be used to create an outline for written communication.

4 Professional image

4.1 Corporate image

Written communications may be the first or only contact people have with you in a business situation – and first impressions count! A letter or email is like an 'ambassador' for you, your organisation and your department.

Key term

> **Corporate image** is the image of itself which the organisation seeks to project to the outside world.

In order to convey professionalism, the presentation of your message should show the following qualities.

- If handwritten, it should be legible (readable), neat and free of excessive visible errors and corrections (such as crossings out or Tippex). Neatness and legibility are the absolute minimum requirement in a professional context. Do not compromise on this!

- It should demonstrate competence in using word-processing or email software, and whatever tools you are using (including the use of diagrams).

- It should demonstrate some regard to the needs of the user, such as clear diagram labelling, cross-referencing of appendices, and citing of information sources.

- It may even display some features of good 'design', such as creative use of space, and the use of devices such as <u>underlining</u>, **bold** or *italic* type, for headings and emphasis.

Communications also create or reflect the image that outsiders have of an organisation: its **corporate image**. Your organisation may seek to project itself as creative, youthful and informal – or as reliable, mature and traditional. Your communications should reflect that image, and there may be **corporate identity** and house style guidelines to help you in doing this. You may, for example, be instructed to include corporate logos; to use specially designed letter, memo or email stationery; to use particular layouts, colours or typefaces; and/or to include certain standard elements (such as blocks of text accompanying your signature at the bottom of letters and emails).

If such guidelines exist – follow them.

Activity 2: Word processing

Which of the following are advantages of using a computer word-processing package for producing business documents and communications?

Tick the boxes which are advantages.

	✓
Documents can be saved and edited easily.	☐
They provide the personal touch.	☐
The writer can make corrections and changes which are 'invisible' to the reader.	☐
Documents can be tailored to individual circumstances but this takes time – often quicker to write from scratch.	☐
Standard or 'template' documents can be created.	☐

4.2 Personal image

A person's appearance can be a part of conveying a corporate image, in line with the organisation's objectives, as well as conveying the individual's image.

Organisations may advise staff on areas such as clothing, cleanliness, body language or verbal language. Practicalities are a consideration as much as image, as, for example, it is not useful to wear formal clothes while digging a ditch, or to wear dirty clothes in a bakery. However, an organisation may require, or even provide, badged or designed clothes in a corporate image.

The personal image may help to make a person appear more professional, and therefore competent. There may also be practical benefits such as making a person more identifiable in a retail situation where customers and staff are mixed. As an individual the image may make an impression on colleagues and managers.

Non-verbal communication can be conveyed by the subtleties of body language, even when the individual concerned is not aware of it. Body language is where thoughts, intentions or feelings are expressed by physical behaviours, like facial expressions, body posture, gestures, eye movement, touch and the use of space. Being aware of these factors enables a person to convey a desired image, for professional or social needs.

5 Business relationship needs

5.1 Good business

A successful business is more than just the assets and liabilities shown in its accounts. In many cases its main asset can be said to be its staff, whose effectiveness can depend on personal skills leading to good relationships. These skills should also be used to create good relationships with external stakeholders like customers.

If a customer respects and trusts their supplier's staff they are more likely to order repeatedly, rather than just once. The creation of this relationship can depend on staff behaviour and their personal qualities.

5.2 Formality

Styles of communication range from extremely informal and friendly through to extremely formal and impersonal. It is important that the right style is used in appropriate contexts!

There is the basic requirement that **any** business communication must be courteous, businesslike and professional. This does not necessarily mean 'formal': if you work in an organisation where all levels of employees and managers are on first-name terms, the style of communication will tend to be less formal than in an organisation where all managers are addressed by their title and surname, eg as Mr Jones or Ms Smith.

Even in relatively informal settings, however, the appropriate style for business communication will be significantly more formal than you might use in a note, email or text message to a friend. You **must** bear this in mind – both at work and in your assessment!

Formality expresses respect for the position and professionalism of the person you are dealing with, and signals the seriousness with which you take your own work role. Formality is also important in getting your message across, since many people find text message style abbreviations and slang terms not just disrespectful and unprofessional – but also difficult to decode!

Therefore it is better to write in full, grammatical sentences, avoiding abbreviations, and abbreviated forms such as 'there's' or 'we've' (the full forms 'there is' and 'we have' are preferable). Your language should be direct (not ambiguous), accessible (but not clichéd) and factual (not too emotional or 'colourful'): avoid colloquial or slang expressions. You should keep to the point and avoid unnecessary digressions. Your tone should be appropriate for business relationships: not overly 'familiar' or friendly in tone, or personal in content, and referring to people by their title and surname – unless they have expressly invited you to be more informal.

5.3 Personal attributes

Everyone may be born with different character traits, and in many cases can develop them during life. Some of these personal qualities will be useful in a business context, as in the examples at the start of the chapter. However, the circumstances of different job roles may require them in varying degrees. Consider that someone working in accounts may need to handle money, and confidential information. For a receptionist, an important factor will be meeting the public, including customers.

Activity 3: Job description

Southfield Electronics is aiming to recruit a new Telephone Sales Assistant.

Categorise the following personal qualities as 'E' for essential, 'D' for desirable, or 'N' for not necessary for the role.

Aggressive	
Assertive	
Good communicator	
Good listener	
Introvert	
Respectful	
Responsible	
Trustworthy	

Activity 4: Business style

Allocate *(assessment style: Drag and drop)* the Do's and Don'ts of acceptable business style into the appropriate columns.

Do...	Don't...

The drag and drop choices are:

Write in full sentences

Refer to people by their title and surname, in more formal relationships – or where their expectations about formality are unknown

Use direct, commonly used and factual language

Use colloquial or slang expressions

Use 'text message' style abbreviations

Remove digressions, rambles and unnecessary words and phrases: keep to the point

Be overly 'familiar' or friendly in tone, or personal in content, unless the other person has expressly invited this

Use abbreviated forms such as 'there's', 'I'm', 'we've': use the full forms ('there is', 'I am', 'we have') instead

---

6 Numeracy skills

You should already have been developing your numeracy skills in your studies for other units, such as *Bookkeeping Transactions*. So you won't be starting from scratch in preparing to demonstrate your competence in this assessment!

The important thing here is to recognise when your numeracy skills are being called on, select the right techniques and tools to use – and apply them carefully and accurately.

6.1 Addition and subtraction

Addition is used in sub-totalling and totalling amounts: columns of debits and credits, for example, or itemised costs, or the total output of team members, or an amount payable after the addition of VAT.

Subtraction is used for operations such as calculating net pay after deductions, or amounts payable after deduction of a discount.

Addition and subtraction should, with practice, be a fairly straightforward operation (with or without a calculator). However, you do need to think carefully about whether you are selecting the right items or numbers to add or subtract, from a list of data.

6.2 Multiplication and division

Multiplication is used in operations such as calculating annual costs from monthly costs (multiplying by 12), or calculating total costs from unit costs (cost per unit multiplied by the number of units). It is also used when dealing with fractions and percentages of an amount.

Division is used in operations such as calculating the cost 'per' unit (total cost divided by number of units).

Multiplication and division should, similarly, become a fairly straightforward operation with practice (although in this case, a calculator certainly helps). Again, however, you need to think carefully about whether multiplication or division are required, and which items of data to select for the operation. We will look at some practical examples in a moment.

6.3 Fractions

A **fraction** is a ratio of two numbers. ¼ means 'one part in four': it also means 1 **divided** by 4.

To find 'a fraction of' something, you simply use multiplication. Say the cost of 20 invoiced items is £360, but you only ordered and received 8 items. You need to work out the cost of 8 out of the 20 items.

$8/20 \times £360 = £144$

When working with fractions (especially if you aren't using a calculator), it helps to use the simplest version of the fraction, with the lowest numbers. You can do this by a process called 'cancelling down': simply divide the top and bottom numbers of the fraction by the same amounts, until they won't go any further.

Because fractions are ratios or relationships, they stay the same as long as you multiply or divide the top and the bottom numbers **by the same amount**.

$$\frac{8}{20} = \frac{4}{10} = \frac{2}{5} \qquad\qquad \frac{24}{30} = \frac{12}{15} = \frac{4}{5}$$

In these examples, you might like to stop cancelling down at 4/10 – or use equal top and bottom multiplication to convert 4/5 into 8/10, because tenths are very easy to work with, and easy to convert into decimal points (8/10 = 0.8) and percentages (8/10 = 80/100 = 80%).

If you are using a calculator, you will need to familiarise yourself with the 'fraction button' (if any) and how it is used.

Illustration 2: Using and converting ratios

You are investigating inaccuracies in the work of the Accounts section at Southfield Electronics. You have been told that 3 out of every 12 invoices in the section's work contain an error, and you want to calculate how many errors that makes over a whole day's work of 88 invoices.

You could rephrase the problem as follows.

$$\frac{3}{12} = \frac{?}{88} \quad \text{Cancelling down:} \frac{1}{4} = \frac{?}{88}$$

What do you have to multiply 4 by to get to 88? Division is the reverse operation to multiplication, so you work backwards: $88 \div 4 = 22$. Now you know you have to multiply the bottom of the fraction by 22 and, in order to keep the ratio the same, you have to do the same to the top.

$$\frac{1 \times 22}{4 \times 22} = \frac{22}{88}$$

If 3 out of 12 invoices are faulty, then – at the same rate of errors – 22 out of the daily total of 88 invoices may be faulty!

There is another way of thinking about this. You could say that 3/12 or ¼ (one-quarter) of all invoices have an error. 3/12 of 88 invoices is calculated as:

$3/12 \times 88 = 22$

So 22 invoices out of 88 will have an error.

6.4 Percentages

A **percentage** is a proportion or rate per hundred parts (per cent). It is used to express any proportion in relation to a whole: fractions can also be expressed as percentages, by multiplying by 100.

$$\frac{1}{4} = \frac{100}{1} = \frac{100}{4} = 25\% \qquad \text{or} \qquad 0.25 \times 100 = 25\%$$

Percentages are quite easy to calculate, using multiplication.

$$4\% \text{ of } 900 = \frac{4}{100} \times 900 = 36 \qquad \text{or} \qquad 0.04 \times 900 = 36$$

The same method can be used to calculate:

- The amounts of VAT (20% of a total amount) to be added to an invoice, or the amount of a percentage discount (say, 10% of a total amount) to be deducted from a total cost.

- The size of segments of pie charts, and other relative proportions (eg the percentage of total training costs incurred by a particular training programme).

- Changes (eg in sales, costs or output) from one period to another. If your Accounts department processed 288 invoices in March and 300 invoices in April:

$$\text{Its output grew by } \frac{300 - 288}{288} = \frac{12}{288} \times 100 = 4.2\%$$

Activity 5: Calculations

A particular training programme costs £2,300. Your department's total training budget is £11,500. Answer the questions below, entering each answer to the nearest whole number.

(a) What percentage of the total budget is represented by this training programme?

[＿＿＿＿＿＿] %

(b) If you were to draw a pie chart showing this percentage, how many degrees (of a 360-degree circle) would it represent?

[＿＿＿＿＿＿] degrees

(c) If your department was eligible for a 15% discount on all training programmes over a value of £2,000, what would be the amount of the discount, and what would be the net amount payable?

Amount of discount   £ [＿＿＿＿＿＿＿＿]

Net amount payable   £ [＿＿＿＿＿＿＿＿]

6.5 Rounding

Rounding is a way of making numerical data easier to use by reducing the accuracy (or detail) of numbers to an appropriate level. If you are compiling **average** numbers of trainees on courses, for example, it may not be helpful to talk about 6.8 trainees being away from work at a given time: it would make more sense to round up to 7 (whole) trainees!

Similarly, if you have 7 trainees on courses costing a total of £699, and were asked for the 'cost per trainee', you know that you need to divide the cost by the number of trainees – and your calculator will tell you that you get £99.8571428. This is not particularly digestible or helpful information – particularly since, in monetary units, you really only need two decimal places to give you pounds and pence.

To round to 2 decimal places, just look at the 3 numbers after the decimal place: in our example, 857. We are looking to round to the nearest 10, and this means rounding up to 860 (since 57 is closer to 60 than to 50). We can then knock off the final zero, to give us £99.86.

To round to 3 decimal places, look at the 4 numbers after the decimal place: 8571. We can round down to the nearest 10 (because 71 is closer to 70 than to 80): this gives us 8570 – and we can knock off the zero for the rounded number £99.857.

Illustration 3: Using percentages (VAT)

Back at Southfield Electronics, you have been asked to do some VAT calculations. You know that these calculations require the use of percentages, fractions, multiplication, division, addition, subtraction and rounding – so you are determined to work through the calculations carefully.

The net amount (sales price) shown on one invoice is £235.46. How much VAT should be charged on this amount? You know that VAT is 20% of the sales price and is rounded down to the nearest whole pence.

$$20\% \times £235.46 = \frac{20}{100} \times £235.46 = £47.092 \text{ (rounded to £47.09)}$$

The total amount (including VAT) will therefore be:

$$£235.46 + £47.09 = £282.55$$

On another invoice, you see that the gross amount (the total price of goods plus VAT) is £375.80. How much VAT is included in this price, and what is the net price of the goods? The total price includes the added 20%, so it totals 120% of the net price. The VAT is, of course, 20% of the total price. So:

$$VAT = \frac{20}{120} \times £375.80 = £62.6333 \text{ (rounded to £62.63)}$$

To get the net price of the goods, you then subtract the VAT from the VAT-inclusive price: £375.80 – £62.63 = £313.17.

Activity 6: Invoice

Goods with a list price of £2,450.00 are to be sent to a customer. The customer is allowed a trade discount of 15% and VAT is to be charged at 20%.

What is the invoice total?

£ [   ]

6.6 Averages

An average is another way of reducing the level of detail in numerical data to a usable level, based on finding a value that is 'typical' or representative of a larger set of data.

There are three different types of averages.

- The **arithmetic mean** is found by adding up all the items in the set, then dividing the total by the number of items in the set.

  Say there were the following customer complaints about invoices over a six-month period.

January	February	March	April	May	June
0	26	0	5	3	2

The average number of complaints is:

$$\frac{0 + 26 + 0 + 5 + 3 + 2}{6} = \frac{36}{6} = 6 \text{ per month}$$

The problem with this is that **extremes** (like 26) distort the average: the actual monthly complaints are not as bad as 6 in 5 of the months. The average also disguises the fact that there was a real problem in February!

- The **median** is the middle value, when you arrange the data in ascending order. (If there is an even number of items, the median is mid-way between the middle two.) Here are our monthly complaints, reordered:

0	0	2	3	5	26

↑

Median = 2.5

- The **mode** is the most frequently occurring value in a set of data. So the mode for our monthly complaints is 0.

Activity 7: Averages

You are trying to compare the costs of training courses offered by two different providers, for a Continuing Professional Development plan.

The course costs are as follows.

	Provider 1 £	Provider 2 £
Legal Compliance	250	340
Payroll Procedures	590	375
Spreadsheets	260	290
VAT Update	300	350
Effective Communication	200 per day*	210 per day**

* 3 day course
** 2½ day course

(a) What is the mean value of a course for each provider?

Provider 1 [   ]

Provider 2 [   ]

(b) What is the median value of a course for each provider?

Provider 1 [   ]

Provider 2 [   ]

(c) **Based on your answers to (a) and (b), discuss which provider offers best value in terms of cost.**

6.7 Selecting the right numeracy tool

One of the tricky things about being set numerical tasks is that they are often set in words! You have to work out what numerical operation is required to get the information you are being asked for.

- To calculate work output 'per' month, for example, you need to divide the total output by the number of months under consideration.

- On the other hand, if you are asked to calculate work output in a particular month, you may need to add up the output of different team members in that month.

- If you are told how many tasks a team member can complete in an hour, and the number of hours she worked in a day, you will need to multiply the hours by the hourly output to get her total daily output. You could multiply this by the number of days worked in the month, to get this team member's monthly output.

- If you know the total monthly output and the monthly output of each team member, you could also calculate the percentage of the total monthly output represented by each team member: team member output divided by total output multiplied by 100. For ease of use, you might round this percentage to one or two decimal places. (You could then recalculate them as percentages of a 360° circle and draw a handy pie chart, to motivate the team with a bit of healthy competition!)

- Now, say that a team member's time costs £50 per half day when she is away on a training course, and that she does 1 day of training per month. How would you manipulate this information to calculate the total overtime cost over a year? First of all, notice the different units we've been given to work with: half days, days, months, years. Let's get them all into a common unit: days.

  £50 per half day = £100 per day.
  1 day per month × 12 months in a year = 12 days per year.
  Now it's easy: 12 days × £100 per day = £1,200 per year.

- What if you then found you were eligible for a 10% discount from the training provider because your spend exceeded a particular threshold? You would have to calculate the **percentage** (10/100 × total spend) – and then deduct it from the total.

6.8 Accuracy in numerical tasks

One of the great problems in accounting and payroll work is the need for a high level of accuracy – particularly avoiding silly mistakes such as adding a number instead of subtracting it, using the wrong tables or making an arithmetical error. This is also a problem in assessments! So what can you do to minimise the risk of errors?

- Always check your work before finishing and submitting it.

- Don't see tasks as mechanical processes: try to understand what the numbers represent, so that you know (a) what needs to be done with them and (b) whether answers are plausible or likely.

- Perform credibility checks, such as using mental arithmetic to see approximately what you expect the answer to be.

Activity 8: Percentages

Calculate the cost of each employee's travel expenses as a percentage of the total cost of travel expenses. Calculate the percentage to three decimal places.

	Travel expense £
Anne	45
Jaitinder	71
Benjamin	86
Chloe	32
Vimal	59
	293

Anne		%
Jaitinder		%
Benjamin		%
Chloe		%
Vimal		%

Assessment focus point

Assessment tasks for this topic are likely to cover literacy and numeracy.

A typical literacy task may present paragraphs which need to be checked and incorporated into an email. Attention should be focused on omissions, technical errors and spelling errors.

As an example, consider why the following two sentences do not match:

Errors within communications are not acceptable. As a consequence customers may decide to continue to do business with the organisation.

The absence of a 'not' does make a difference.

For prospective accountants a high level of accuracy in numeracy tasks is expected, and great care should be taken with fractions, percentages, ratios and proportions, where misreading a task can lead to errors.

An example of a common error is where the current year profit of £4,200 shows a 5% increase over the budget. The task may require you to calculate the budget figure. Here it would be incorrect to calculate £4,200 × 5% as the increase is already included in the current year profit. It would be correct to calculate £4,200/105 × 100 = £4,000.

Double check this answer by taking the £4,000 budget and adding 5% (= £200) to get back to £4,200.

Chapter summary

- Communication is, at its most basic, the transmission or exchange of information. It is at the core of the role of the accounting and payroll functions within an organisation.

- You are required to demonstrate that you can communicate effectively, clearly and appropriately in a range of situations. This broadly means using appropriate formats; observing format conventions and house style; presenting information neatly and professionally; ensuring that content is technically correct and clearly understandable (bearing in mind the needs and capacities of your audience); projecting an appropriate corporate image; and achieving your purpose in communicating.

- When planning a communication, you want to PASS: know your Purpose and Audience, and use the right Structure and Style.

- Keep It Short and Simple (KISS) is an important guideline for business communication.

- The formality appropriate for business communication is considerably greater than you might use in non-work settings, and you must bear this in mind.

- You are required to demonstrate a range of numeracy skills appropriate to this level, including (but not limited to) addition and subtraction, multiplication and division, fractions, percentages, and rounding to a certain number of decimal places.

- Other important numeracy skills are (a) working out what numerical operation is required to get the information you are being asked for, (b) checking the accuracy of your calculations and (c) formatting your work in a clear way.

- **Average:** A value that is typical, representative or 'middling' for a set of data

- **Communication:** A method of putting across a message and ensuring that the message is understood

- **Corporate identity:** Guidelines for how the organisation presents itself visually in its communications

- **Corporate image:** The image of itself which the organisation seeks to project to the outside world

- **Fraction:** A ratio of two numbers – for example, ¼ means 'one part in four'

- **Interpersonal skills:** Personal attributes that enable one person to interact effectively with others

- **Jargon:** Technical terminology which may not be understood by non-specialists

- **Percentage:** A proportion or rate per hundred parts – for example, 20% = 20 parts per 100 or 1/5

Test your learning

1 **Complete the following sentence using the picklist below.**

[▼] is the response of a person with whom you are communicating, which indicates whether your message has (or has not) been received and understood as you intended.

Picklist:

Budget control
Exception reporting
Feedback
Feedforward

2 It is 15 May and you have just received an invoice for 2,000 kg of raw materials. Inclusive of VAT (sales tax) the invoice totals £4,580 and the VAT rate is 20%.

Next month you need another 2,000 kg of the same raw material but you know the VAT exclusive material price is set to rise by 3% by the start of June.

What will the VAT value be on the 2,000 kg to be purchased in June rounded to two decimal places?

£ [   ]

3 Your Accounts department processed £16,600 worth of invoices in January and £20,916 worth of invoices in February. **What percentage increase in revenue does this represent?**

[   ] %

4 **What would be the closing salutation in a formal letter where the opening salutations are:**

(a) **Dear homeowner**

(b) **Dear Mrs Melborne**

5 The sales for 20X1 and 20X2 were £480,000 and £552,000 respectively. **What would be the sales for 20X3, assuming that they increase from 20X2 by the same percentage as the last 2 years?** Your estimate should be rounded to the nearest thousand pounds.

Presenting information

Learning outcomes

3.1	**Produce accurate work in appropriate formats**
	• Use standard business communications: business letters, emails, formal business reports, spreadsheets
	• Show how standard business communications are usually structured and presented: business letters, emails, business reports, spreadsheets.
	• Choose the appropriate format to present business information

Assessment context

The presentation of information is an important part of the unit syllabus, and is likely to be examined. The assessment may require the construction of professional informal business reports, letters, emails and memos. The selection of formats relevant to a situation may be tested, and standard formats will need to be used correctly and effectively within organisational guidelines.

Qualification context

Some of the themes of this chapter occurred in the chapter on 'Personal skills', and will reoccur and be developed in the following chapters on 'Working independently' and 'Working as part of a team'.

References to these themes, particularly reports and emails, may be used occasionally in other units in Levels 3 and 4, but not examined specifically.

Business context

Presenting information in a competent and persuasive way is an important part of the finance professional's role. Colleagues, managers and external contacts may be dependent on its understandability, accuracy, completeness and timeliness, for making business decisions.

Chapter overview

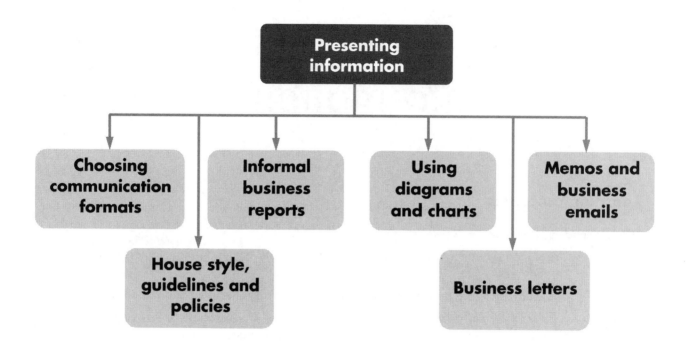

Introduction

In this chapter we look at various methods of communication, and these include emails, memos, and brief reports. We also cover the importance of presenting information in the correct, and most appropriate format for users.

1 Choosing communication formats

There are a variety of possible methods of communication for presenting business information, and you must select the most appropriate method for the circumstances, for the target audience, and for the type of message that is to be relayed.

Face to face communication (in meetings, interviews, discussions or presentations) allows you to express yourself fully, to be sensitive to the other person, to take advantage of on the spot question and answer, and to gain immediate feedback to make sure your message is getting across. However, a face to face meeting is often not possible due to time constraints or physical location. It is also often the case that, particularly with a complex subject, it is better to communicate the details in writing so that the recipient has time to consider the details and complexities and has a copy for reference/confirmation.

If immediate feedback or personal sensitivity is required but face to face communication is not feasible, the next best option is a telephone call.

Short notes are good methods of passing on information and providing a reminder (eg asking someone to carry out a task) in informal settings (eg among colleagues).

Letters are often used in formal, person to person business communication where urgency (given the lead time for postal delivery) is not a factor. Letters can be made confidential by stating 'private and confidential' on the envelope and at the top of the letter, so that only the target recipient should open the message.

Informal reports are often used in business communication to convey larger amounts of information in a clear, structured, easy to use way.

Memos are a standardised, efficient way of sending messages within an organisation. They may be the approved internal format for notes and short informal reports.

Email is extremely versatile: it can be used to send notes, memos, letters, reports, forms and all sorts of other messages. Email has the huge advantages of speed (provided the recipient picks up the message when it is sent) and electronic format (so it can be easily filed, edited, copied and sent to multiple recipients all at once). It can also have other documents (reports, diagrams, schedules and so on) 'attached', if this would be helpful in backing up the main message.

2 House style, guidelines and policies

As we saw in the previous chapter, business communication needs to be more planned, more formal and more efficient than everyday communication, in order to:

- Make best use of the time of all parties involved

- Avoid misunderstandings or communication failures, which could be detrimental to the achievement of deadlines and objectives

- Establish and maintain positive relationships with colleagues, customers, suppliers and other stakeholders in the business

For this reason, organisations often issue guidelines for their staff on how to use various communication methods efficiently and effectively, and how external messages should be presented.

2.1 Communication policies

Organisations often publish policies and guidelines on how to use – and how not to abuse – communication tools such as the telephone and emails.

There may be restrictions on making personal calls or using email and internet for personal purposes at work. There will often be strict warnings about the unacceptability of offensive or illegal content in messages – although we hope this would be common sense! In an accounting and finance setting, there will almost certainly be policies about confidentiality: what information can and cannot be given, to whom, and by what means, to protect the integrity and security of information.

There may also be helpful guidelines for staff about issues such as data security when using email (eg the use of anti-virus software); the rules of email 'etiquette'; when to use (and not to use) email; and what 'signature' information should be added to the end of emails.

2.2 House style

Organisations seek to communicate a consistent, coherent image to the outside world – and, ideally, also one that reflects the corporate identity, self-image and style. If every member of the organisation presents letters and emails differently, according to their own preferences, a consistent image will be difficult to maintain!

'House style' is an expression of how the organisation wants to present itself in its communications. It may include aspects such as the use of standardised letterheads and memo pads; how letters and memos are laid out; what headings and formats are used for reports; and the logos, typefaces and colours used as part of the corporate identity. It may also include more subtle aspects such as a tendency towards informality or formality in the tone of writing, or creativity or traditionalism in the style of presentation.

House style may be developed informally, as 'the way we do things around here', which people pick up through modelling their messages on existing examples. House style may also be formally expressed in guidelines and rules for communication – and if this is the case, in your organisation you should seek to adhere to the guidelines set for you.

Illustration 1: House style

At Southfield Electronics, there is a house style manual for all communications sent to external parties.

Standardised stationery is available for handwritten and word-processed documents – and also for email messages. The corporate letterhead appears as follows.

SOUTHFIELD ELECTRONICS LTD

Tomorrow's technology for today's homes

Micro House
Newtown Technology Park
Innovation Way
Middx NT3 OPN

Every email must be 'signed off' with a standard block of text called a 'signature block', which is inserted automatically by the email software:

[Sender's Name]

[Sender's Position]

Southfield Electronics Ltd
Micro House, Newtown Technology Park
Innovation Way, Middx NT3 OPN, UK

Tel: +44 (0)20x xxx xxxx * Fax: +44 (0)20x xxx xxxx *
Web: www.southfield.com

This message and any attachments are confidential and may contain information that is subject to copyright. If you are not the intended recipient, please notify us immediately by replying to this message and then delete it from your system. While we take reasonable precautions to prevent computer viruses, we cannot accept responsibility for viruses transmitted to your computer and it is your responsibility to make all necessary checks. We may monitor email traffic data and the content of emails to ensure efficient operation of our business, for security, for staff training and for other administrative purposes.

2.3 General guidelines for effective written communication

We have already looked at these in the last chapter: be ready to apply them to specific formats such as reports, letters, memos and emails. In order to create clearer communications and foster more effective working relationships:

- Take into account your purpose in writing: what are your aims and objectives? What response or action do you want as a result of your message?

- Take into account the requirements of your target recipient or audience: their information needs and capacities (including their limited time, and familiarity/ unfamiliarity with technical jargon)

- Structure your communication in such a way as to make it easy to read and understand

- Keep it short and simple (KISS) and aim for clarity and ease of understanding

- Present your material in a way that demonstrates professionalism and reflects the desired image of the organisation

We will now look at some of the main tools for presenting information in the accounting and finance environment.

3 Informal business reports

'Report' is a general term, which covers a wide range of formats. If you inform someone verbally or in writing of facts, events, actions you have taken, or suggestions you wish to make – you are reporting. In this sense, you can make a report in a meeting or phone call, letter, memo or email.

If you are asked for an informal report, however, this will usually mean a relatively short written document, in which information is presented in a direct and structured way.

3.1 Informal report structure and style

A formal report can be a massive, complex and highly structured affair, presenting and analysing high-level concepts and information. An informal report is generally used for less complex reporting tasks, so it does not require elaborate referencing, structuring and layout. However, it still needs to have a clear structure and layout, to help the user to 'navigate' through the information.

There are some important points to note about the written style of an informal business report.

The language is still more formal than that used in everyday speech, or in informal messages to colleagues. Avoid slang and colloquialisms. Write grammatically in full sentences. Do not take short cuts: use 'there is' rather than 'there's', and 'I have' rather than 'I've'.

The key objective is ease of understanding, and ease of navigation through the information, for the user. A good report will:

- Avoid technical language for non-technical users
- Organise material logically – especially if it is designed to be persuasive, leading up to a conclusion or recommendation!
- Signal relevant topics by using appropriate headings
- Use tables or diagrams, where this would be helpful in highlighting important points (such as comparisons or trends), or in organising raw data (eg into a table)
- Include background or supporting detail into an **appendix** or appendices: attaching relevant documents at the end of the report, in order to keep its main body concise and flowing

Key term

Appendix is a term for a separate section attached to a report, with supporting data or documents referred to in the report.

There are seven key sections of an informal report you need to know about for the assessment. These are as follows.

- Title (or title page)
- Executive summary (sometimes just referred to as the summary)
- Introduction
- Main body/detailed findings (divided into a series of meaningful subsections)
- Conclusions
- Recommendations
- Appendices (as mentioned above)

Now we will look at what each section includes and how a report might look.

REPORT TITLE ('Report on [topic]')

To: Requester/recipient of the report

From: Compiler/writer of the report

Date: Date of submission

Executive summary

The executive summary (or summary) should be a short overview setting out the main findings of the report along with a summary of the key conclusions and recommendations. Although presented at the start, it is often written last as this is the best time to assess what the most important 'headline' points are.

Introduction

The introduction should explain the contents, purpose and scope of the report, along with any relevant background information.

Findings (main body)

Then comes the main body of the report which contains the detailed results, findings or observations. This will be structured in sections, with clear headings. There are different ways of dividing the body of the report into sections, such as:

Section headings: as dictated by the report brief

Report sections may reflect a list of topics you were asked to cover in the report 'brief', or request for information. If you are given a number of issues to report on, it makes sense to use these as your report sections.

Section headings: as dictated by the subject matter

A subject will often have topic areas to provide report headings. You might report on a process, for example, under the headings of its various stages or steps. You might report on data security under the headings of particular security risks (viruses, phishing, systems failure, loss of data).

Section headings: as dictated by the task

If you are asked to investigate an issue, give your findings and make recommendations, it would make sense to have sections headed: Background; Investigation; Findings; Recommendations.

Conclusions

This section will collate the key points arising from each of the preceding sections in the main body of the report, discuss them and explain the conclusions reached as a result. The report brief may not have specifically asked for conclusions, but it will still be helpful to the report user to have at least one overall conclusion including what facts, decisions or options the report has led to. An overview of the key conclusions will be included in the Executive Summary at the start of the report.

Recommendations

There is sometimes a separate section containing any recommendations if not already covered in earlier sections, or to collate all the recommendations in one place. The most important recommendations may also be summarised in the Executive Summary.

Appendices

Supporting data and documents can be attached to the report, where useful. Such documents should be numbered and referred to in the body of the report, so the user can locate the data: eg '... based on September sales forecasts (See Appendix 1)' or '... as set out in the attached Schedule (Appendix 2)'.

Illustration 2: Report layout

You have been at Southfield Electronics for a while now, and you are becoming frustrated by the tendency for staff members to 'cut corners' on organisational policies and procedures, such as correct authorisation of cheque requisitions; respect for the confidentiality of other staff members' personal details; and attendance at fire evacuation drills.

You mention this in conversation with Jenny Faulkner, the Financial Accountant, and she asks you to observe and record any further instances over the next month and to write an informal report covering incidences of non-compliance, reasons for concern, and how Southfield can improve compliance. Having observed further non-compliance throughout August 20X0, you draft the following to report the non-compliance to Jenny:

SOUTHFIELD ELECTRONICS LTD

REPORT: COMPLIANCE WITH POLICY & PROCEDURE

Executive summary

During August 20X0 there have been a number of cases where staff members have not complied with company policy, including staff submitting incorrect cheque requisitions, breaches of confidentiality and lack of participation in fire drills. This culture of non-compliance jeopardises efficiency, employee safety and data security. The situation can be remedied by reminding staff of company policy, better staff training and increased monitoring and enforcement of employee compliance by managers.

(1) Introduction

This report sets out observations of non compliance with organisational policies and procedures in August 20X0. It was compiled by Your Name, Accounts Clerk, at the request of Jenny Faulkner, Financial Accountant, and submitted on 23 September 20X0.

(2) Non-compliance with policies and procedures

In August 20X0, I witnessed several cases where staff members failed to comply with formal policies and procedures.

- Cheque requisition forms have had to be returned to the originators because they were incorrectly completed or authorised. (See copies attached: Appendix 1.)

- There is an apparent lack of respect for the confidentiality of other staff members' personal details, in verbal and written communication with third parties. In some cases staff members' details have been provided to third parties by colleagues without obtaining the relevant employee's permission.

- A number of staff members failed to take part in fire evacuation drills. Those that did take part failed to comply with proper procedures (for example, by taking lifts and leaving fire doors open). (See the Safety Officer's report on the most recent drill: Appendix 2.)

(3) **Reasons for concern**

The 'lapses' in compliance are of concern, for several reasons.

Policies and procedures, such as the ones mentioned, have been put in place to ensure the efficiency of operations such as cheque requisition; the confidentiality of information which may be used to the detriment of the organisation and/or its staff; and the safety of staff and visitors in the event of an emergency.

(4) **Conclusions**

Non-compliance in such areas jeopardises efficiency (by necessitating re-work), data security and personal safety.

By themselves these may be small things, but I have come to the conclusion they reflect a culture of 'corner cutting' which may eventually result in more serious consequences and immediate action is needed.

(5) **Recommendations – How Southfield can improve compliance**

I would like to make the following recommendations for management's consideration.

- All staff should be reminded of their responsibility to comply with organisational policies and procedures.

- Where necessary, training should be given to reinforce awareness and competence in relevant procedures.

- Managers at all levels should seek to monitor and enforce compliance more strictly, and to model compliance in their own conduct.

I hope this information is helpful, and I would be willing to discuss it further – and to present more detailed evidence of my observations – at your convenience.

Appendix 1: Incorrectly completed cheque requisition forms (attached)
Appendix 2: Safety Officer's Report for August 20X0 (attached)

4 Using diagrams and charts

If you are preparing a report (or perhaps preparing slides for a presentation), you may need to use visual aids of some kind. Diagrams are useful in conveying large amounts of data more accessibly and in adding interest and appeal to a document.

In addition to the numerical competences required to organise your data, there are some key principles of effective 'graphic' communication.

- Give each diagram or chart a concise and meaningful title.

- Cite the source of the data, where relevant.

- Clearly label all elements of the diagram, either on the diagram itself or in a separate 'key' to the colours or symbols used.

- Keep textual elements (labels, explanatory notes) brief.

- Keep the presentation as simple as possible: cut down on unnecessary lines and elements, to avoid overcrowding, clutter and confusion.

- Make the diagram large enough so that it is easy to read.

Let's look briefly at some examples of visual elements you might use in an informal report.

4.1 Tables

Tables are a good way of organising information. The use of columns and rows allows the data to be classified under appropriate headings, clearly organised and labelled, totalled up in various ways (across rows or down columns) and so on.

You might use a table format to organise data about a list of trainees, say, as follows.

Staff member	Training undertaken	Training provider	Duration of training (days)	Cost of training
John				
Amy				
Fred				
		Total:		

4.2 Bar charts

Bar charts are useful for showing or comparing magnitudes or sizes of items: for example, sales revenue or expenditure on a month by month basis, or training costs per department.

- The diagram needs to be labelled to indicate what it shows.

- The positions of the bars are labelled to show what they represent (eg months or departments).

- The height of the bars, drawn against a specified scale, indicate the magnitudes of the different items (monetary value or number).

- The bars can be subdivided to show components of the total magnitudes (eg breakdown of monthly expenditure by department or category).

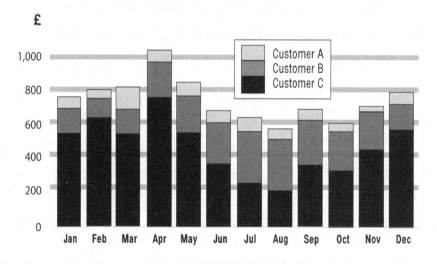

4.3 Pie charts

Pie charts are useful for showing the relative sizes of component elements of a total value or amount, represented by the 360 degrees of the circle or 'pie'. An example might be showing the breakdown of the time you spend on different tasks during a day, or the breakdown of monthly sales revenue by product or customer. Below are the steps involved in providing a pie chart in relation to this.

Step 1 Calculate each item as a fraction and/or percentage of the whole. (If handling emails takes you 5 hours out of your 40-hour week, say, that's 5/40 or 1/8 or 12.5%.)

Step 2 Translate each fraction/percentage into fractions of a circle. (The 'slice' occupied by handling emails would be 1/8 of the pie.) If you want to draw very accurately, using geometric instruments, you would calculate the exact number of degrees of the circle occupied by each slice, as a fraction or percentage of 360° (1/8 × 360°= 45°).

Step 3 Draw a circle, and divide it up using the fractions (or, to be more accurate, degrees) calculated for each slice.

Step 4 Label each slice with what it represents, and its percentage of the total. Check that it adds up to 100%!

Illustration 3: Pie chart

Jenny Faulkner has asked you to report on the breakdown of your 40-hour working week, to check whether your being a 'shared resource' for the Assistant Financial Accountants and Payroll Manager is working.

You work out that in an average week, emails take 5 hours (12.5%); your work on payroll takes 20 hours (50%); and your work on ledgers takes 15 hours (37.5%). In presenting this data in your report to Jenny, you decide it will be most helpful in graphic form. You calculate as follows.

$5/40 \times 360$ = $45°$ (1/8 of the pie)
$20/40 \times 360$ = $180°$ (1/2 of the pie)
$15/40 \times 360$ = $135°$ (3/8 of the pie)

You draw the following simple pie chart, for inclusion in your report.

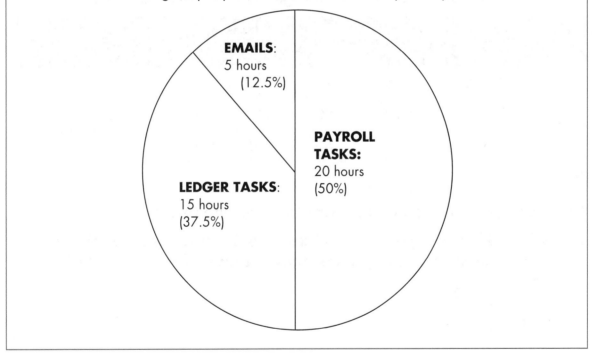

4.4 Line graphs

Line graphs are useful for showing the relationship between two variables (represented by the horizontal and vertical axes of the graph), by plotting points and joining them up with straight or curved lines. These are particularly useful for demonstrating trends, such as the increase in departmental output as more time/money is invested in training and development – or fluctuations in revenue or expenditure (or other values) over time.

Here's a very simple example.

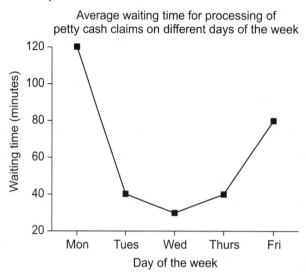

Average waiting time for processing of
petty cash claims on different days of the week

Such a graph could be used to highlight variations in work throughput.

Activity 1: Graphs and charts

The table below shows a company's sales figures for the first six months of 20X0.

Product	Jan £000	Feb £000	Mar £000	Apr £000	May £000	Jun £000	Total £000
A	800	725	725	400	415	405	
B	210	210	180	150	175	160	
C	25	50	60	95	125	140	
Total							

(a) Add up the rows and columns to insert the totals.

(b) What kind of graph or chart would you use to show the fluctuations of monthly sales figures across the six months?

Picklist:

Bar chart
Line graph
Pie chart

Have a go at drawing the graph.*

(c) **What kind of graph or chart would you use to show the proportion of total sales represented by each product?**

Picklist:

Bar chart
Line graph
Pie chart

Have a go at drawing the graph.*

*Note that you will not be asked to produce a graph/chart in the assessment. However, drawing these graphs for this task will aid your overall understanding of when and how to use each particular graph/chart type.

---

5 Business letters

A letter is a very flexible and versatile medium of written, person to person communication. It can be used for many business purposes: requesting, supplying and confirming information and instructions; offering and accepting goods and services; conveying and acknowledging satisfaction and dissatisfaction (eg complaint and adjustment letters); and explaining what else is in an information package via a covering letter.

The modern business letter contains various standard elements and you will need to know what these are and where they are located on the page. Below, you will see a skeleton format and a full example.

Letterheads (the logo, name and contact details of the organisation sending the letter) are often pre-printed on office stationery, or built into word-processor templates. If not you should reproduce the name and address details given at the top of the letter page.

A letter should include:

- The name and address of the target recipient
- The address of the sender
- Date
- Greeting (or 'salutation')
- Subject heading (a brief, helpful 'cue' to what the letter is about)
- An opening paragraph
- The main body of the letter
- A closing paragraph
- Sign-off (or 'complimentary close')

- Signature: if an assistant is signing a letter on behalf of the writer, the writer's name must be preceded by 'For' (or its equivalent from legal terminology: 'pp' which stands for *per procurationem*)

- Enclosure reference: 'enc' (or 'encs' for more than one item), if something other than the letter is included in the same envelope – such as a cheque, price list or leaflet

- Copy reference: 'copies to' or 'cc' plus the names of any third parties to whom copies of the letter have been sent

---

ORGANISATION LETTERHEAD
(may be pre-printed on stationery)

(includes sender's address)

Confidentiality warning (*if applicable*)

Recipient's name
Designation
Address   Date

Greeting (salutation),

Subject heading

Introductory paragraph: explaining the context and reason for writing.

The main body of the letter, set out with clear separate paragraphs for each sub-topic or new phase of your message.

The content may be tackled in chronological order (if you are narrating or explaining a sequence of events, say) or in any other appropriate order for the subject matter.

Closing paragraph: summarising the content and purpose of the message, and making clear what course of action (if any) you want the reader to take. Putting this last makes it most impactful and memorable.

Complimentary close (matched to the salutation),

Author's signature (handwritten)

Author's name
Author's position

Enclosure reference (*if something is in the envelope with the letter*)
Copy reference (*if a copy of the letter has been sent to another person*)

SOUTHFIELD ELECTRONICS LTD

Tomorrow's technology for today's homes
Micro House
Newtown Technology Park
Innovation Way
Middx NT3 OPN

Confidential

J M Bloggs
Administrator
Wallend Retail Ltd
Wood Lane Industrial Estate
Sussex BN1 4PW

3 September 20X0

Dear Mr Bloggs,

Account No 0139742

Thank you for your letter of 28 August 20X0 regarding credit payments owing to your account as a result of product returns.

I have looked into the matter that you raised and I am afraid that your earlier letter of 26 July was indeed overlooked, due to the temporary absence of the member of staff to whom you addressed it.

I apologise for the delay in processing your credit payment. I have arranged for your account to be credited with the sum of £346.99, and I enclose a printout of your account status confirming the balance.

If you have any further queries, please do not hesitate to contact me.

Yours sincerely,

Your Name

pp Kellie McDonald

Assistant Financial Accountant

enc.
cc: Kellie McDonald

5.1 Appropriate salutations

You need to demonstrate that you can use an appropriate greeting or salutation for the type of relationship you have with the person you are writing to: this may be formal or informal, in recognition of the other person's status, the familiarity of the relationship, and the customs of the organisation (such as calling managers by their first names – or not!).

By convention, the following greetings (or 'salutations') and sign-offs (or 'complimentary closes') should be used together, and you need to demonstrate that you can match them correctly.

Salutation	Close	Context
Dear Sir/Madam/Sirs (name not used)	Yours faithfully	Formal situations Recipients not known
Dear Dr/Mr/Mrs/Ms Bloggs (formal name used)	Yours sincerely	Established relationships Friendly but respectful (eg with superiors, customers, suppliers)
Dear Joe/Josephine	Yours sincerely Kind regards	More personal, informal relationships (eg with colleagues)

Activity 2: Letter

You have been asked to write a letter to the following people.

What salutations and closes will you use?

(a)   The Accounts department of a firm you are dealing with for the first time.

Salutation [   ]

Close [   ]

(b)   A female customer whose name you know to be Georgia Brown, but whose marital status you do not know.

Salutation [   ]

Close [   ]

(c)   A sales representative called Mark Stein, whom you know well and with whom you are on first-name terms.

Salutation [   ]

Close [   ]

(d) **The Managing Director of your firm, whose name is Sir Joshua Holmes.**

Salutation [   ]

Close [   ]

5.2 Professional image

A letter may be the first contact a person has with your organisation, so it needs to make a positive impression. As discussed in the last chapter, this generally means: legibility, neatness, conciseness and businesslike tone. If a letter is handwritten, you will need to minimise crossings out (or Tippex). If it is word processed, it will still require attention to spelling errors, 'typos' and other problems (such as faint or blotchy printing) which may spoil the image of professionalism you are trying to create.

5.3 House style

An organisation may have its own stationery and letterhead. House style or custom may also dictate where the standard letter elements are arranged on the page.

- Our example shows what is called a 'semi-blocked' layout, with the date at the top right-hand side of the page, and the subject header centred.

- You will often see the simpler 'fully blocked' style, with everything against the left-hand margin.

At work, you should follow the layout used in your own organisation.

5.4 Well structured

A letter (and indeed any written message) should have a beginning, a middle and an end.

- The opening paragraph is important, because the reader will not be as familiar with the context or reason for the letter as you are! Offer a brief explanation of why you are writing, an acknowledgement of relevant correspondence received, and other introductory background details.

- The middle paragraph(s) should contain the substance of your message. If you are making several points, start a new paragraph with each, so that the reader can digest each part of your message in turn.

- The closing paragraph is important, because it is the best opportunity to make clear to the reader what you hope to have achieved. Summarise your point briefly, or make clear exactly what response is required.

Activity 3: Opening lines

Suggest some opening lines for the following letter situations.

(a) You are replying to an agreement you made by phone to send someone a brochure detailing your services.

(b) You have had a phone message from one of your sales reps, George Brown, saying that a person wants to enquire about job openings in the Accounts department, and would like to be contacted by mail.

Suggest some closing lines for the following letter situations.

(c) You already have a meeting scheduled to discuss the matter further.

(d) You have just provided the person with answers to questions.

5.5 Clearly written

Again, remember the KISS principles we discussed earlier in this chapter. Your written style needs to be helpfully structured (in well-spaced paragraphs), easy to read, unambiguous, free of jargon, free of cliché (without meaningless 'stock' phrases), and concise (without unnecessary words).

We can't really teach you to do this. You will have to develop your skills at letter writing by modelling your style on the examples given in this Course Book – and by evaluating what does and does not work in the letters you encounter.

Assessment focus point

If in the assessment look out for task instructions to see if a letter presentation is required. If so, then always use the layout and presentation style we have looked at in this section on business letters. Use any information given to you in the task to include in your letter, this can include names and addresses (of both you and the recipient!) along with appropriate salutations and a date if this is supplied.

6 Memos and business emails

6.1 Memos

A memo or 'memorandum' performs the same function internally as a letter does in external communication by an organisation. It can be used for reports, brief messages or 'notes' and any kind of internal communication that is most easily or clearly conveyed in writing.

Memos are generally written on stationery pre-printed with appropriate headings – or typed into a word-processor template. The standardised headings are designed to make writing more efficient, given that the message is for internal use.

The following shows the standard elements of memo format.

MEMO

To: [Recipient's name, designation] Reference: [File reference]
From: [Sender's name, designation]   Date: [In full]
Subject: [Concise statement of main theme or topic of message]

The main text of the memo is set out in correct, concise, readily understandable English, in spaced paragraphs following a clear, logical structure. Note that no inside address, salutation or complimentary close are required.

Signature or initials [optional]

cc: [To indicate recipient(s) of copies of the memo, if any]
enc: [To indicate accompanying material, if any]

Nowadays, memos have generally been replaced by internal email messages, which have much the same features – except that you are typing into an electronic form created by email software.

Illustration 4: Memo

Following your informal report on non-compliance with Southfield Electronics' policies and procedures, Jenny Faulkner has been investigating, and one morning you receive the following memo.

SOUTHFIELD ELECTRONICS LTD

MEMO

To: Your Name, Accounts Clerk
From: Jenny Faulkner, Financial Accountant
Date: 11 September 20X0
Subject: Abuse of telephone procedures

I have been looking into instances of non-compliance with procedures, and I believe I have identified an additional matter that would be worth investigating further. As you know, our telephone costs have risen significantly over the last quarter, and I have identified three main causes.

(1)   There are more telephones in the office than are necessary for efficient communication.

(2)   Staff have become accustomed to making personal calls on office apparatus.

(3)   Many calls are made at expensive charge rates and at unnecessary length.

I would like the accounts team to come up with some ideas for action to prevent further cost increases. Is this something that you might be interested in taking on as a project?

Meanwhile, let me know if you have any initial thoughts on the matter.

Thanks.

JF

Activity 4: Memo and letter

Using blank paper complete the following two business communications.

(a) Write Jenny a brief memo replying to the memo sent to you in Illustration 4 above.

(b) Write a brief letter to an office equipment company (TeleComs Ltd, 6 Park Way, Brighton, Sussex BN3 4PW) asking for information about models and costs of electronic switchboards and devices for the logging of telephone calls from handsets.

6.2 Email

Email is a method for sending electronic messages from one computer to another, either internally within the workplace or to an external party. Email is easy to use, extremely fast and relatively cheap. It is also particularly flexible, because photos, diagrams, computer files or spreadsheets can be sent (with the email as a kind of 'covering letter') as attachments.

To use email, you simply log onto the email software (one of the most common being Microsoft Outlook), and press 'Create email' or 'New email'. This presents you with a standard email 'page', which looks a bit like a memo form with extra option buttons!

If you have access to email facilities, you simply type data into the fields on the on-screen email page. When the recipient receives your message (and/or when you print it out), the various headers will be included in the printout, and the sender address and date will be inserted automatically.

You may be asked to complete an email in an assessment task by entering the recipient's email address and selecting appropriate words based on accompanying information.

The standard elements for an email are much like a memo.

EMAIL

To: [Recipient's email address: name@company.co.uk or similar]
Cc: [Email addresses of parties to whom the message is copied]
From: [Sender's email address]
Date: [Today's date]
Subject: [Concise statement of main theme or topic of message]
Attach: [Name of file attached to the message]

The main text of the email should be written in correct, concise, readily understandable English, in spaced paragraphs following a clear, logical structure and a simple format – avoid the use of **bold**, underlined, *italic* or CAPITALISED text (capitals in an email give an impression of you shouting, which is not professional).

Name/initials (optional)

Signature block (inserted automatically, if used)

6.3 Using email effectively

Email is so widespread, it is easy to forget that it has some limitations as a medium of communication!

It is not as secure as you might think (particularly if you accidentally send it to the wrong address or multiple addresses): think carefully before using it for private and confidential messages.

Email is fast and easy to use: think carefully before 'dashing off' messages which may damage relationships (eg by being offensive or inappropriately informal) or have practical implications (eg making commitments to a customer or supplier which you can't later fulfil).

As some email programs remove formatting, it is best to avoid anything fancy in an email that you send, such as **bold**, <u>underlined</u>, *italic* or CAPITALISED text, since these may not actually be seen by the recipient. Also to be avoided because of the unprofessional impression they give are 'emoticons' such as smileys: ☹.

When you have finished the message, always check it through thoroughly: once it has been sent there is no retrieving it!

You should familiarise yourself with the email format (and any guidelines for use) of your organisation.

Assessment focus point

Keep it professional! There can be a temptation to send informal chatty emails to colleagues but in the assessment keep your email communications formal and businesslike and avoid unnecessary abbreviations or the use of textspeak in emails – this applies to both internal and external email messages!

6.4 Making best use of the subject line

The subject line is more or less compulsory in emails (sometimes the software won't let you send a message without one) because, if you don't signal what the message is about, the recipient may think it is spam (an unsolicited mass marketing message) or some kind of fake message carrying a computer virus: any message without a relevant subject line should be deleted unread!

The subject line is helpful in letting the recipient know whether the message is worth reading; whether it is high or low priority; and whether it has been directed to the right person (or needs to be forwarded). It also directs the recipient to the subject of the message, like a very brief 'executive summary', so that he/she can be mentally prepared, and read the message more efficiently.

So use the subject line wisely. Use a short phrase that will most effectively convey the seriousness, relevance and topic of the message to a user who may not be expecting it. ('Hi there' or 'read this' probably won't do the job...)

If you are replying directly to an email sent to you (by pressing the 'reply' button), the email software will insert the subject line: 'RE: [the subject of the original message]'. So if you reply to a message 'Monthly totals', the subject line will automatically read: 'RE: Monthly totals'.

Illustration 5: An email

Back at Southfield Electronics, you are working on your analysis of the customers that have been allocated to you. Just to check that you are doing it correctly, you would like a copy of an analysis which your colleague Amy Laval has already completed. A possible email to Amy requesting the analysis could be as follows.

EMAIL

Date: [inserted automatically]
To: alaval@southfield.co.uk
From: yname@southfield.co.uk
Subject: Customer analysis

Amy,

I'd be grateful if you could send me a copy of a customer analysis that you have already completed, so that I can check that I am doing it correctly.

Thanks.

Your Name

Activity 5: Email

Using blank paper compose an email from Amy to you, in reply to your email to her in Illustration 5 above.

Assessment focus point

Assessment tasks for this topic are likely to require completion of an email and compilation of a report.

A typical task may present data to be checked and inserted into an email or other form of communication. Even the more basic step of entering the correct email address should be carefully considered. Care should also be taken in selecting paragraphs to insert that are appropriate, and in the correct order.

Another typical task may require an email, or report, to be proofread. Much attention is needed to be paid to grammar, spelling and writing protocols. You should read the document at least twice – once straight through to understand the whole, and again reading one sentence at a time with attention to detail.

A third example may describe a scenario, and require that relevant conclusions and recommendations are selected for a report. Here it is important to know and understand the seven key sections of an informal report, mentioned earlier.

- Workplace communication methods include face to face discussion, telephone calls, informal notes, memos, emails, letters and informal reports.

- Organisations often issue guidelines for staff on how to use various communication methods efficiently and effectively, and how external messages should be presented. 'House style' is an expression of how the organisation wants to present itself in its communications, and house style conventions and guidelines should be adhered to, to ensure consistency and coherence.

- Informal reports are relatively short written documents, in which information is presented in a direct and structured way. They should follow a clear logical structure, and be written in an easy to understand and appropriately businesslike (relatively formal) style.

- Diagrams and charts (including bar charts, line graphs, pie charts and flow charts) may be used in reports to illustrate key points of data. They should be carefully drawn and labelled for ease of use.

- Business letters are highly versatile for person to person written communication. They contain various standard elements. You will need to know what these are and where they are located on the page in different 'house style' layouts. It is particularly important to use appropriate salutations (greetings) and closes.

- Memos cover a wide range of internal written messages. They are generally written on stationery with pre-prepared standard headings.

- Email is a method for sending a written message from one computer to another. Email software, like memo stationery, has pre-prepared headings into which you can input sender/recipient and subject information. You need to make good use of the subject line.

- Regardless of format, all reports, letters, memos and emails must conform to house style guidelines and the attributes of effective communication.

Keywords

- **Appendix:** A separate section attached to a report, with supporting data or documents referred to in the report

- **Email:** An electronic method of sending a note, letter, memo or other information via computer

- **House style:** The distinctive way an organisation seeks to present itself in its communications

- **Informal report:** A relatively short written document, in which information is presented in a direct and structured way

- **Memo:** A structured message sent within an organisation via internal mail

1 **For each of the following situations, which would be the most appropriate method of communication? Choose from the picklist below.**

Situation	Method
Detailing a telephone message left by a supplier for a colleague	▼
Informing an employee that his work has not been up to standard recently	▼
Requesting a customer's sales ledger account balance from the credit controller	▼
Requesting production details for the last month from the factory manager where the factory is situated five miles away	▼
Sending monthly variances to the sales manager	▼

Picklist:

Email
Face to face discussion
Informal note

2 **What information is usually contained in the three sections of a report shown below (on the left-hand side)? Indicate your selections by drawing lines between the relevant information (on the right) and the section in which it would appear (on the left).**

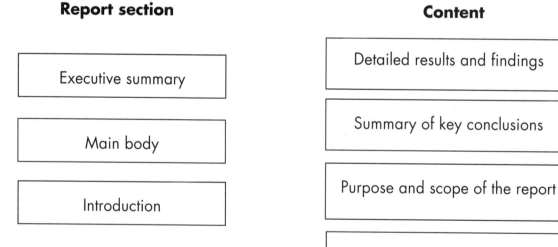

Report section

Content

Executive summary

Main body

Introduction

Detailed results and findings

Summary of key conclusions

Purpose and scope of the report

Overview of key findings

3 A fellow member of your AAT local branch recently asked you for advice on report writing, and specifically on the use of appendices. **Draft a short letter (making up appropriate details of your and the other person's address) explaining the purpose of an appendix, and what they need to do to ensure that they use appendices effectively. Use a fully blocked letter layout.**

4 **Select the grammatically correct sentences from those below:**

(a)	When we asked our most trusted customers for feedback, they say they want later opening hours.
(b)	When we asked our most trusted customers for feedback, they said they want later opening hours.
(c)	When we asked our most trusted customers for feedback, they said they wanted later opening hours.

5 **Select the grammatically correct sentences from those below:**

(a)	An increase in working hours will have a major affect in staff wellbeing.
(b)	An increase in working hours will have a major effect on staff wellbeing.
(c)	An increase in working hours will have a major effect in staff wellbeing.

6 **Select the grammatically correct sentences from those below:**

(a)	The company's presentation is full of great idea's, and it get's right to the point of it's strategy.
(b)	The company's presentation is full of great ideas, and it gets right to the point of its strategy.
(c)	The company's presentation is full of great ideas, and it gets right to the point of it's strategy.

Working independently

5

Learning outcomes

3.3	Plan workload to meet the needs of the organisation
	• Understand the importance of communicating with others during the completion of tasks or when deadlines are in danger of not being met
	• Understand the importance of meeting agreed deadlines and adhering to working practices
	• Be able to work independently, and manage workload using time-management techniques and planning aids
	• Be able to plan, prioritise, monitor and review workload within deadlines.

Assessment context

Working independently is a significant part of the unit syllabus, and is likely to be examined. The assessment may require the review of task deadlines, and drafting of personal planning schedules, to ensure they are met.

Qualification context

Some of the themes of this chapter, such as meeting deadlines, will overlap with the chapter on 'Working as part of a team'. Understanding the role of the finance function, in an earlier chapter, will be relevant to planning task completion.

The themes in this chapter may be referred to generally in other units in Levels 3 and 4, but not examined specifically.

Business context

Being able to plan and manage your own workload is an important quality for the finance role. It involves issues such as prioritising, flexibility, confidentiality and meeting deadlines which enable you to make an effective contribution to a business. The range of planning aids and organisational tools considered will be relevant to most businesses.

Chapter overview

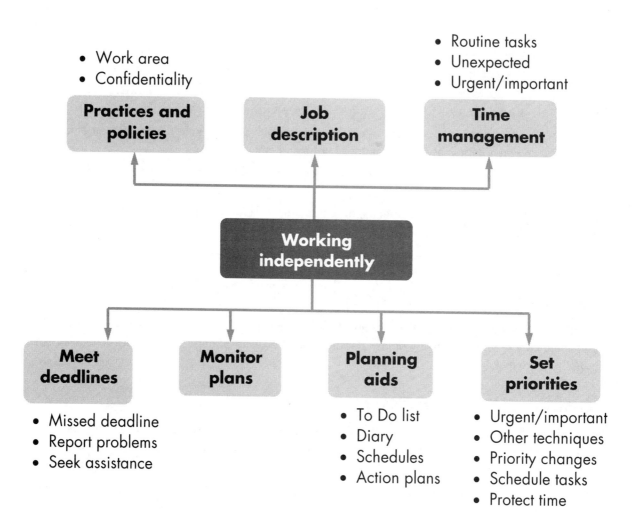

- Work area
- Confidentiality

- Routine tasks
- Unexpected
- Urgent/important

Practices and policies

Job description

Time management

Working independently

Meet deadlines

Monitor plans

Planning aids

Set priorities

- Missed deadline
- Report problems
- Seek assistance

- To Do list
- Diary
- Schedules
- Action plans

- Urgent/important
- Other techniques
- Priority changes
- Schedule tasks
- Protect time

Introduction

Our fifth chapter looks at various techniques that can be used to help prioritise tasks, and meet set deadlines. This chapter also looks at the correct approach when there is a risk of a deadline not being met.

1 What is involved in a job?

A 'job' is a collection of tasks and responsibilities allocated to an individual. Some organisations allocate a defined set of tasks to individuals in particular positions, while others allow teams to allocate tasks among themselves more flexibly (within the constraints set by the team's goals and targets for performance).

1.1 Job description

A key element in being able to work effectively is knowing exactly what is required of you (and what you are not necessarily expected to do). In most cases, an employee will be given a **job description** when they enter a position. This should include a job title and an outline of the main tasks and responsibilities involved in the job.

Illustration 1: Job description

When you started work at Southfield Electronics, you were given the job description shown below.

JOB DESCRIPTION

Job title: Accounts Clerk, financial accounting
Location: London office
Job summary: General financial accounting duties

Key responsibilities:

- Providing administrative and clerical support to the Assistant Financial Accountants and Payroll Manager, including filing, answering the telephone and dealing with post

- Undertaking work as requested, including: obtaining quotes from suppliers; preparing daily cheque listings, sales invoices, credit notes and monthly sales summaries; and checking purchase invoices to goods received notes

- Using own initiative to deal with enquiries in the absence of the Assistant Financial Accountants

- Being aware of the importance of maintaining strict confidentiality in all aspects of work

---

Reporting structure:	Financial accountant | Assistant Financial Accountants (2) and Payroll Manager | Accounts Clerk
Hours:	9:00am to 5:30pm Monday to Friday 1 hour for lunch
Training:	Induction training will be provided Continuing Professional Development encouraged
Prepared by:	Head of HR
Date:	March 20X0

2 Time management

Time is a resource – the same as money, information, materials and equipment. You have a fixed and limited amount of it, and various demands in your work (and non-work) life compete for a share of it. If you work in an organisation, your 'time is money': you will be paid for it, or for what you accomplish with it.

Time, like any other resource, needs to be managed if it is to be used efficiently (without waste) and effectively (productively).

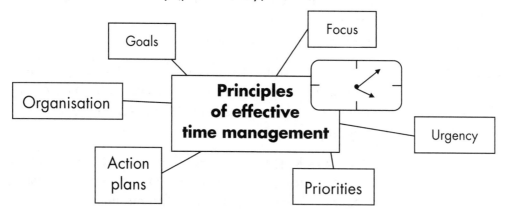

The key principles of **time management** (Adair, 2009) can be summarised as follows.

- **Set goals** for all aspects of your work, so that you know what you want to achieve – and can tell when you have done so.

- **Formulate action plans** that set out how you intend to achieve your goals: the timescale, deadlines, tasks involved, resources required and so on. (We will look at various **planning aids** later on.)

- **Set priorities**: decide which tasks are the most important – what is the most valuable use of your time at this moment? – and list them in the order in which you would tackle them. (We discuss how to do this below.)

- **Focus**: give your attention to one thing at a time, if possible. Make sure that everything you need for the task is available, avoid interruptions if you can – and then concentrate.

- **Urgency**: do not put off tasks because they are difficult or large. (They will only get worse as the deadline approaches!) Work on any task you are doing as if it were urgent.

- **Organisation**: develop positive work habits which minimise the time and effort spent (and wasted) on tasks. Do similar tasks (eg photocopying) in batches to avoid multiple trips to the photocopier. Keep your filing up to date, so you know where to find things. Manage your in-tray: don't let things 'pile up' without dealing with them or making a plan to do so.

2.1 Routine tasks

Much of your day at work will revolve around carrying out **routine tasks** that will have been summarised in your job description. Some of these will be daily tasks, such as opening the post, doing the filing and dealing with incoming emails. Other tasks may be weekly tasks, such as paying suppliers' invoices, or monthly items, such as preparing the bank reconciliation statement.

Illustration 2: Tasks to do

Every day at Southfield Electronics, you are (as stated in your job description) required to open the post in the morning. You have to list any cheques received from customers and give the cheque listing to Kellie McDonald. If any purchase invoices are received from suppliers, you retain them for checking against 'goods received' documentation during the week. Once checked, you hand them over to Kellie McDonald each Friday morning for payment.

You distribute any other post received to the in-trays of the relevant people each morning.

During each day, you will receive despatch notes from the Stores department, for goods which have been sent out to customers. Each day, you are required to prepare sales invoices corresponding to these despatch notes, which are then sent to the Financial Accountant, Jenny Faulkner, for checking by the end of each day: they are then sent out to the customers the next day.

You will also receive goods returned notes from the Stores department. By the end of each week, you must have produced, and sent to Jenny Faulkner, a credit note for each goods returned note.

At the end of each month, Jenny Faulkner requires a listing of all invoices and credit notes sent out during the month.

A number of times per week, you will receive purchase requisitions which have been authorised by Jenny Faulkner. Your task is to email the appropriate suppliers, requesting quotations, and to prepare purchase orders from approved suppliers.

All copy invoices, credit notes, purchase invoices and purchase requisitions should be filed each day.

As office junior, you are also (informally) expected to ensure that there is tea, coffee, milk and biscuits in the office kitchen.

In order to keep track of all these routine tasks, you could summarise them in a helpful format, as follows.

Daily	•	Open post
	•	Prepare cheque listing
	•	Distribute other post
	•	Check emails and respond
	•	Prepare sales invoices
	•	Filing
	•	Check kitchen supplies
Weekly	•	Check purchase orders – ready for Friday morning
	•	Send quotation requests and purchase orders
	•	Prepare credit notes
Monthly	•	Prepare sales invoice/credit note listing

2.2 Unexpected tasks

As well as the general, routine tasks that are part of your role, you may be asked to perform non-routine or unexpected tasks. These may be one-off special jobs, cover for an employee who is off sick, or assisting a colleague to complete their task. They may also include the handling of enquiries or queries from customers, suppliers or other staff members.

Such tasks are part of general working life, and you will need to fit them into your work schedule. This is why the guidance notes for this unit refer to 'changing priorities as appropriate': in other words, adjusting your plans and priorities to take account of changing demands.

Activity 1: Routine or unexpected

Place each of the tasks below in the relevant box using the picklist below.

Routine tasks	Unexpected tasks

Picklist:

Dealing with petty cash as the petty cashier is off sick
Listing cheques received in the post each morning
Preparing a special report for your manager
Performing the weekly bank reconciliation
Preparing sales invoices daily
Showing a visitor around

2.3 Urgent tasks and important tasks

Some tasks will be **urgent tasks**: they need to be completed for a **deadline** in the near future. For example, the Marketing Director may request a breakdown of sales by product for a meeting first thing tomorrow morning.

Other tasks might be classified as **important tasks**. These are jobs that have major value or potential consequences for the organisation: for example, preparing cost estimates for a major purchase, or a report for a high-level meeting. A task will be classed as important if:

- Other people or tasks rely on its timely completion (a task which is relatively unimportant to you may be an important part of someone else's work);

- The consequences of non-completion are high (in terms of costs, damage, delay); and/or

- It has been requested by an individual or body which has high power (eg a senior manager or government agency).

It is natural to think that an urgent task is important – or that an important task is urgent – but this is not necessarily the case. You may have time to devote to the important task – or you may have to 'drop' an urgent task because it is not as important as another requirement. This is a question of priority.

Activity 2: Urgent or important

It is the first day of the current month.

Indicate whether each of the following tasks is urgent or important. (Select urgent if you think the task is both urgent and important. If the task is important but not urgent, select important.)

Task	Important/Urgent	
Preparing a credit note listing for your manager due by the end of the month		▼
Producing a staff analysis for the Personnel Director for a meeting this afternoon		▼
Producing product costings for the Production Manager for a meeting first thing tomorrow morning		▼
Checking purchase invoices to goods received notes		▼

Picklist:

Important
Urgent

3 Setting and managing priorities

Even with routine tasks, it may be necessary to plan the order in which you will carry them out on a given day or week. When unexpected tasks are introduced as well, this form of planning becomes even more important. The process of determining the order in which tasks should be carried out is known as **prioritising**. So how do you go about it?

3.1 Prioritising by urgency and importance

Clearly, urgent tasks are higher priority than non-urgent tasks, and important tasks are higher priority than unimportant tasks. You might therefore use a simple framework, like the Eisenhower Decision Matrix (Covey, S. 1990), with four categories:

Urgent and important	Tasks that must be done in the very near future and which are important to you and to other people in the organisation. (For example, you are asked to produce a report for a manager for a high-level strategy meeting tomorrow morning.)
Not urgent but important	Tasks which are important but not immediately due. (For example, today is Monday and the project manager has asked for some product costings for Friday.) Beware, however; if you leave non-urgent tasks too long, they become urgent!
Urgent but not important	Tasks which are urgent – but will not be a major problem if not completed in time. (For example, there is no milk in the kitchen, and the shops are about to close. The worst that can happen is some grumbling, until you can find time to shop the following morning.)
Not urgent and not important	Tasks that can be slotted into the gaps between higher-priority tasks. (For example, periodically you may pack up out of date files to be stored in the archives.)

Illustration 3: Non routine tasks

As well as your routine duties at Southfield Electronics (detailed earlier), you discover that a number of other tasks are required of you today, Thursday, when you come into work.

- There is no milk in the fridge, and it is your responsibility to replace it.

- Jenny Faulkner has left a note on your desk saying that she needs the November sales figures by lunchtime, for a meeting with the Managing Director.

- Kellie McDonald requires photocopies of the cheque listings for the last two weeks by Friday lunchtime.

Remember that you also have your routine duties to carry out. How should you plan your day? To start with, you could categorise your tasks according to their urgency and importance.

Category	Tasks	Comments
Urgent and important	Open and distribute post Produce daily cheque listing Check emails **Plus November sales figures (today)**	Although the routine tasks are not as important as the job for Jenny, they are still important: your colleagues rely on you completing them.
Not urgent but important	Prepare sales invoices Check purchase invoices ready (Fri) Check credit notes prepared **Plus copy cheque listings (Fri)**	There should be time to fit these in around the urgent/important tasks – but keep an eye on them, because they will become urgent if left too long.
Urgent but not important	**Buy milk**	May be important to colleagues, so perhaps persuade one of them to do you a favour (in their own interests) and go to the shop!

Your day can now be organised with the tasks undertaken in the order suggested by the above analysis.

3.2 Other prioritising techniques

If tasks are of equal urgency and importance, or there are no particular issues of priority, the following are some other possible criteria for determining the order in which tasks should be completed.

- Arrival time: performing tasks in the order in which they are requested.

- Most nearly finished: starting with the task nearest completion. (It is satisfying ticking off finished tasks – and frustrating to interrupt a nearly complete task to start something else.)

- Shortest task first: enabling you to get lots of tasks out of the way quickly.

- Longest/most difficult task first: enabling you to get some momentum on tasks you might otherwise procrastinate over!

- Difficulty of handover: if you are about to go on holiday, say, you should tackle the things that it will be most difficult for someone else to take over while you are away.

Activity 3: Prioritising

It is 4:00pm on Friday afternoon and the office will shut at 5:30pm. You are in the process of printing off the sales invoices for the day, to be checked by the accountant and sent out this evening. Your supervisor approaches you and asks you to print out and bind a confidential report that she requires for a meeting on Monday at 12:00 noon. There is only one printer in the Accounts department. You estimate that there are still another 30 minutes of sales invoice printing, and that the high resolution report will take about two and a half hours to print and bind.

Which of the following actions should you take now?

Continue printing the sales invoices ☐

Interrupt the sales invoice printing in order to
print the confidential report instead ☐

In the assessment you could be provided with a number of work requests and deadlines, which you would then have to prioritise and organise in order to ensure that they will all be completed on time.

3.3 Dealing with changes in priority

Just because you have planned your tasks for a day or a week does not mean that they are fixed in stone! As other unexpected tasks come along, you may well need to change your priorities – and therefore the order in which you carry out your jobs.

Illustration 4: Change in priorities

You have been working hard in the Financial Accounts department at Southfield Electronics this Thursday morning and by 11:30am, you have produced the November sales figures for Jenny, opened the post, prepared the cheque listing and distributed the post. You also managed to persuade Amy Laval to go out and buy the milk. However, you are just about to check your emails when Jenny Faulkner comes over to your desk.

She tells you that Sam Piper, the new Accounts Assistant, has gone home ill. One of Sam's most urgent tasks today was to prepare statements for two large customers who are querying the amount that they owe. As you have done this before, Jenny asks you if you will perform this task for Sam and get the statements to her by 4:00pm for checking and sending out in the post tonight.

You now have to change your priorities, as this task is both urgent and important. Your day will now look as follows.

- Prepare customer statements by 4:00pm at the latest
- Check emails – deal with any that are urgent
- Photocopy the cheque listings for Kelly McDonald
- Prepare sales invoices for the day
- Check that purchase invoices will be ready for Friday morning
- Check that all credit notes have been prepared

A pretty full day!

3.4 Scheduling tasks

Once you have a list of priorities, you will need to **schedule** tasks, by determining when you will tackle them.

Key term

Schedule is the allocation of tasks to appropriate times or dates when a task will be tackled or completed.

Determining the time that it will take to do a task is easy if it is a routine procedure that you have done many times before: simply note how long it takes you, on average. With non-routine tasks, particularly substantial ones, it can be far more difficult to determine how long to allow. You can ask someone with more experience than you, or you might be able to break the task down into smaller stages whose duration you can more easily estimate. The important thing is to be realistic!

Time schedules can be determined by different methods.

- Forward scheduling: adding the estimated duration of each task from its scheduled starting time/date, to give you the target completion time/date. This is useful for scheduling routine tasks.

- Backward scheduling: subtracting the estimated duration of each task from its deadline or completion time/date. This gives you the latest start from which you'll get the job done in time – so schedule an earlier start where possible! This method is useful for meeting deadlines and for complex tasks, where each stage depends on the timely completion of the previous stage.

- Slotting your tasks into appropriate start dates/times, in order of priority – and fitting lower-priority tasks around higher-priority ones. Remember to check that your daily schedule only adds up to the number of working hours in your day (allowing for lunch breaks, routine daily jobs and scheduled meetings). Tasks which don't 'fit' can then be moved to a bigger 'slot' (if they have to be done all in one go) or carried over for completion on another day.

Activity 4: Scheduling tasks

An accounts assistant works from 9:00am to 5:00pm (with a lunch break between 1:00pm and 2:00pm). The assistant has the following routine daily duties which are listed in order of priority below (most important shown first) with the maximum expected duration of the task shown in brackets.

- Respond to customer queries from the day before (1 hour)
- Enter sales invoices/credit notes (45 mins)
- Enter purchase invoices/credit notes (45 mins)
- Enter cash receipts and payments (1 hour)
- Print daily cheque run (30 mins)
- File all sales and purchases invoices and credit notes (1 hour)

On arriving at work on Thursday, the assistant notices two messages on her desk.

- The first is from the Accountant asking for a statement to be generated and sent via email to a major customer as soon as possible. It will take a maximum of 30 minutes to complete this task.

- The second is from the HR Manager asking the accounts assistant to attend a compulsory meeting for all employees to take place in the HR office at 3:30pm, expected to last an hour.

At 2:00pm the assistant picks up an email from the Managing Director asking for the balances and recent activity on the accounts of eight customers which he urgently requires for a meeting at 9:00am tomorrow.

The director says extracting this information will probably take about one hour, but the assistant is more familiar with the computer system and is almost certain the task will take an hour and a half.

Using the picklist below, indicate the order in which the accounts assistant should have carried out the tasks for the day.

Thursday tasks		Order of task completion
	▼	First task
	▼	Second task
	▼	Third task
	▼	Fourth task
	▼	Fifth task
	▼	Sixth task
	▼	Seventh task
	▼	Eighth task

Picklist:

Enter cash receipts and payments
Enter purchase invoices/credit notes
Enter sales invoices/credit notes
File all sales and purchases invoices and credit notes
Generate eight customer balances for MD meeting
Generate statement and send to major customer
HR meeting
Print daily cheque run
Respond to customer queries from the day before

3.5 Protecting your time

In addition to planning your time, time management requires you to control – and sometimes protect – your time, in the face of changing and competing demands.

- You may need to delegate less important tasks which can be done by other people, in order to free up your time for more important tasks which only you can do.

- You may need to develop skills in assertiveness (stating clearly, firmly but calmly what you feel, need or want), in order to ask for help when you need it – or to say 'no' when others inappropriately make demands on your time.

We look at this, in the context of working as part of a team, in Chapter 7, but it is important to remember that if a colleague or manager tries to add something to your planned and agreed schedule, this may cause a conflict of priorities, and you will have to negotiate solutions to such conflicts. As we have seen, the solution may be to reprioritise your schedule, if it is flexible enough, or to ask for assistance or extra time where necessary.

However, it may be that the only solution is to say 'no' to requests, if they are unreasonable. In a professional setting – and particularly if the requester is in a position of authority – this will have to be done courteously and positively (proposing alternative ways of getting their demands met if possible), but also firmly.

4 Planning aids

There are a wide variety of planning aids that can help you to ensure that all of your tasks are remembered, scheduled, monitored and completed on time.

4.1 To Do list

The simplest planning aid is a 'To Do list', tick list or checklist. Here you simply write down each task that is required of you for the day, preferably in prioritised order. Then as each task is completed, you tick it off from the list – the satisfying part!

At the end of the day, anything left unticked on the To Do list can be carried over to tomorrow's To Do list and fitted into tomorrow's tasks and priorities.

Another advantage of this technique is that, if you have to hand your tasks over to someone else, it is easy for them to see where you are 'up to'.

4.2 Diary or timetable

The purpose of the diary or timetable is to slot events, tasks or meetings into clearly labelled time 'slots' (hours or days), where they become an easily used reminder (and signal that that time is 'taken' and cannot be used for other scheduled items).

Diaries also offer a useful follow-up system, because you can schedule questions, checks and follow-up actions: for example, to check that you have received the data you requested on the day it was due.

Diaries and timetables can be paper-based or electronic (eg using a PDA, electronic personal organiser, mobile phone or computer). Software such as Microsoft Outlook and Palm Desktop is often used to combine a diary, alarm clock (notifying you of the time for diarised events), To Do list (with reminders as you approach deadlines) and address book (in case you need to contact other people involved).

You might like to experiment with such tools if you have access to them. The limitations of such systems are: they do not guarantee efficient or organised working; it is easy to grow dependent on them (to the point where loss or damage creates chaos); and they can take quite a lot of time to use effectively!

4.3 Planning schedules and charts

Schedules and charts are often used for more complex tasks or projects. They tend to be used when a project involves a number of separate tasks, some of which must be completed before others can be started. Longer-term planning schedules may be conveniently set out using charts or monthly/yearly 'planners'.

Bar charts are often used to 'block out' periods of time on a calendar, to show when tasks are scheduled, or when staff members are on holiday. This has the advantage of clearly showing where tasks fall in the month/year, what order they fall in, where they overlap and so on.

A **planning schedule** is a form of bar chart, but each division of space represents both an amount of time and an amount of work to be done in that time. Lines or bars drawn across the space indicate how much work is scheduled to be done and/or how much work has actually been done.

This makes it easy to measure your progress, and whether you are ahead of schedule or behind schedule. Here's an example of a planning schedule for a small furniture maker, showing work in progress against schedule at the morning break time on Thursday 8 March 20X0.

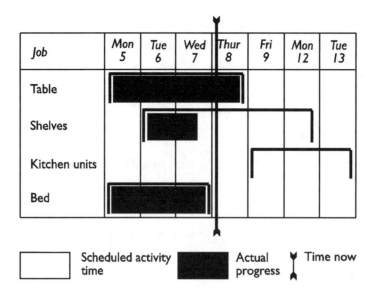

Job	Mon 5	Tue 6	Wed 7	Thur 8	Fri 9	Mon 12	Tue 13
Table							
Shelves							
Kitchen units							
Bed							

☐ Scheduled activity time   ■ Actual progress   ⅄ Time now

Activity 5: Planning chart

What can you tell from this planning chart about the furniture maker's progress on the scheduled tasks for the week?

Choose from the picklist below:

Table ▼

Shelves ▼

Kitchen units ▼

Bed ▼

Picklist:

Ahead of schedule
Behind schedule
Completed on schedule
Not due to start

Illustration 5: Scheduling tasks

Management Accountant Kate Saltmarsh has to produce the quarterly cost accounts for the quarter ending 30 November for the Finance Director by Monday 13 December. From experience she knows the following:

- Once she has all of the information to hand, it will take her two full days (around her other tasks) to produce the accounts.

- She will need a variety of information from the Assistant Management Accountants and this will take them two days to prepare.

- The typing of the accounts can be done in half a day and then there will be another half day of proofing and checking.
- The accounts must be sent to the general office for binding which will take a further day.

If Kate is to have the accounts on the Finance Director's desk by the morning of Monday 13 December, she will have to start work some time in advance. So she draws up a To Do list, backward scheduling based on having the accounts fully bound at close of business on Friday 10 December.

To do list
- Friday 10 December – binding
- Thursday 9 December – typing and proofing
- Tuesday 7 and Wednesday 8 December – preparation time
- Friday 3 December – request information from assistants

Kate then realises that she will be out of the office all day on Tuesday 7 December, and will need to allow for this as well. The final planning schedule for the preparation of the cost accounts will therefore be as follows.

December	Thu 2	Fri 3	Mon 6	Tue 7	Wed 8	Thu 9	Fri 10
Request information	■■						
Preparation of accounts			■■		■■		
Typing and proofing						■■	
Binding							■■

From this Kate will also be able to warn the typist to be ready for the work on Thursday 9 December, and warn the general office to be ready for the binding task on Friday 10 December.

Activity 6: Timetable

At the end of Friday 5 October, your in-tray includes a number of work requests for the following week. You collate them to draw up a To Do list. (The 'job codes' are the initials of the person who requested each task, plus a number, so that you can slot them into a timetable more easily.)

Job code	Task	Approx time	Deadline (end of:)
AB1	Project cost analysis	7 hours	Wed 10
AB2	Depreciation figures	5 hours	Wed 10
AB3	Presentation slides	8 hours	Thu 11
AB4	Check inventory (stock) figures	12 hours	Mon 15
Train	Training course	6 hours	Fri 12: 8am–3pm
AB5	Collect staff CPD plans	2 hours	Fri 26
CD1	Check statements	6 hours	Tue 9
EF1	Aged receivables (debtors)	6 hours	Tue 9
EF2	Bank reconciliations	4 hours	Mon 8

(a) Complete the timetable that follows, indicating what task you will work on for each hour of each working day. (Note that overtime has been authorised for a maximum of two hours each day.)

(b) Identify any task(s) where you may have difficulty meeting the deadline.

TIMETABLE					
	Mon 8	**Tue 9**	**Wed 10**	**Thu 11**	**Fri 12**
[8:00–9:00]					
9:00–10:00					
10:00–11:00					
11:00–12:00					
12:00–13:00					
13:00–14:00					
14:00–15:00					
15:00–16:00					
16:00–17:00					
[17:00–18:00]					

Task(s) carried over to week beginning 15 October:

•

•

4.4 Action plans

An **action plan** is an even more detailed planning tool which can be used for complex and usually longer-term projects. It contains a considerable amount of detail and is monitored on a regular basis to ensure that things are going to plan and, if they are not, to devise how the situation can be rectified. An action plan normally contains:

- Details of each task which is part of the project
- Start date of each task
- Completion date for each task
- Person responsible for each task
- (In some cases) expected and actual costs

5 Monitoring plans

Plans are all well and good – but things do not always 'go to plan'! It is important that schedules are monitored to ensure that everything is happening as and when expected. If not, adjustments may have to be made either to how the task is being done (if extra effort or resources are required) – or to the plan or deadline (if it was unrealistic, say).

All individuals must maintain checks and controls over their work, to ensure that stages of work are 'on track', that jobs have in fact been completed at the deadline (or payments made when they fall due), and that agreed follow-up actions are not forgotten.

Checklists are useful for monitoring what has been done and what hasn't. Diary systems may also be used. Some computer-based organiser systems issue alert messages when the scheduled event or completion time approaches.

You should keep copies of work plans and schedules, and any work request forms (or other communications in which you are asked to perform tasks). This will enable you to:

- Check that your work is on track with your current schedule

- Review and keep track of original work requests, plans and priorities, as the situation changes

- Monitor the need for follow-up action

- Review your scheduling and workload management, perhaps with your supervisor or learning coach, to see how effectively you have translated work requests into plans and schedules

6 Meeting deadlines

A deadline is a set or agreed time when a task must be completed. It is important to realise that deadlines are set for a reason. Some are obvious reasons: the sales director has a meeting with a large customer this afternoon, say, and needs a

printout of the sales to this customer for the last six months. The time of the meeting is the (obvious) deadline.

Other reasons for deadlines may not be so obvious. Your line manager has asked for some figures for Wednesday, because she has to write a report for Monday morning: you don't necessarily know that it will take her two days to complete the report – but she does.

6.1 Missing deadlines

If you fail to complete the task by the deadline, this will affect the person who has asked you to undertake the work – and has then relied on you to do so.

There may be occasions when it will become apparent that you are going to struggle to meet a deadline. This could be for a number of reasons.

- Your workload may be too great for you to finish on time.

- Colleagues who are providing you with required information may have failed to meet their deadlines for doing so.

- You may not have planned effectively or worked efficiently enough.

- Unexpected, higher-priority demands may have been placed on your time, pushing lower-priority tasks back.

6.2 Reporting problems in meeting deadlines

Whatever the reason, if you become aware that you may not meet a deadline you must report the fact immediately to the appropriate person. This may be the individual who has requested the work, your supervisor or line manager, or a colleague who is relying on the work.

It is never easy to admit to someone that you are not able to complete a task on time, but it is important that you do so as soon as you anticipate difficulties.

- The person expecting the work may find that if you miss your deadline, they will miss theirs – and they will need time to adjust their plans or warn others.

- A manager may be able to take action to enable you to meet your deadline.

This second point is particularly important. Provided that you report any anticipated difficulties in meeting a deadline early enough, there are actions that can be taken to help! The manager can:

- Put pressure on any other employees who are holding you up by not producing the information you require

- Lighten your existing workload in order to free up time to meet the deadline

- Provide you with additional resources, such as extra computer time or another colleague's time

- Adjust plans, so that you will have more time

6.3 Seeking assistance with problems

The first stage is to recognise that you are not going to be able to complete the assignment without some additional help. Be prepared to admit this to yourself, if necessary!

When you ask for assistance, try to identify what resources you require: extra time to get the task done yourself, say – or additional computer time or help from a colleague.

If you are in a position to delegate work to more junior team members, they may provide the extra resources required. However, in many cases you will have to approach a more senior manager or colleagues and request assistance. You will need to explain why you need the assistance and what you think is required.

You may need to negotiate: persuading the other person to help you, by showing how it will benefit them, or by offering something they want in return.

Once you have been granted assistance, it is important that it is in fact a help – not a hindrance! Helpers need to be properly briefed on what is required. At the same time, assisting you should not become a burden or disruption to the other person's work.

7 Adhering to working practices and policies

We discussed some of the legal, policy and procedural requirements for accounting and payroll – and why it is important to adhere to them – in Chapters 2 and 3.

It is important to adhere to any agreed working practice, even if it is just 'customary', because other people will be basing their plans and conduct on their expectation that you will do so. If you depart from accepted procedures and practices, you are creating a risk of disruption to plans and damage to working relationships – as well as, perhaps, risks to health and safety, confidentiality, the integrity of data and so on: all the things the procedures and practices are designed to protect.

7.1 Communicating with your line manager or supervisor

In general, you will need to adhere to instructions and departmental practices for maintaining communication with your supervisor or line manager in a range of situations, including:

- Providing information, and reporting on work progress and results, where this is routine or requested

- Reporting by exception: that is, reporting when there has been some deviation or variance from the plan or budget

- Seeking advice and assistance for decisions or actions beyond your competence to perform effectively

- Seeking authorisation for decisions or actions beyond the scope of your authority to deal with

- Receiving information and instructions, perhaps as part of regular or occasional team briefings

- Seeking and receiving feedback on your work performance

- Seeking learning and development opportunities in your work, eg if your supervisor is willing to act as an on the job coach, or has responsibility for authorising your development objectives and plans

You will need to observe established customs and protocols for how this communication takes place. Your manager may exercise informal 'management by walking around'; you may have defined opportunities for communication (eg in regular meetings, briefings or 'open door' hours); or you may need to put information and queries in writing, using email or memoranda.

7.2 Organising and maintaining your own work area

As we mentioned in Chapter 3, the maintenance of your work area is often the subject of organisational policies, mainly aimed at ensuring that offices maintain a professional image, and reflect the corporate image of the organisation, particularly in areas which are visited by outsiders.

However, it is also your responsibility to organise your work area so that it helps – and does not interfere – with efficient and effective work habits. This might mean:

- Positioning your desk (where possible) to ensure that you have sufficient space for your activities

- Ensuring that you and others can move efficiently and safely around the work area, without obstructions or hazards

- Positioning chairs for visitors, printer tables and filing cabinets for efficient use

- Organising your desktop and shelving to ensure that items you use regularly are within reach – and that your space is generally tidy, so that you and others can easily find items when required. Aids to organisation include document trays, desktop organisers, devices to keep electrical wiring out of the way, pin boards (where you can stick reminders etc) and filing systems

- Ensuring that you tidy away all sensitive and confidential documents (and their computer equivalents) when you leave your desk unattended, and especially when you leave work at the end of the day, in order to protect the security of the data

7.3 Respecting confidentiality

We covered the need for confidentiality (and data security) in Chapter 3, but it is always worth repeating! In order to work effectively in accounting and finance, you must be aware of – and adhere to – all work practices and procedures involving rules of disclosure and non-disclosure, the protection of confidentiality, and the secure handling and storage of sensitive data.

> **Assessment focus point**
>
> The task for this topic will provide one or more work schedules, for example Financial Accounts and Management Accounts, plus additional information, requiring the activities to be scheduled in a set time frame.
>
> Read the information given carefully, ensuring:
>
> - **All** information is considered, including tasks due for completion early next day (so may need to be done end of previous day)
>
> - You are aware of the difference between 'completed by' and 'started by'

Chapter summary

- An employee's job will usually consist of a variety of tasks which may be set out in a job, role or competence description.

- A typical job will be made up of a number of daily/weekly/monthly routine tasks plus other unexpected tasks to which schedules must be adapted as required.

- Tasks can be categorised as urgent or non-urgent and important or unimportant when setting priorities.

- You must be able to deal with changes in priorities and therefore changes to your planned work schedule.

- A variety of planning aids can be used to ensure that all tasks are completed on time: eg To Do lists, diaries or timetables, planning schedules and action plans.

- If it appears that a deadline may not be met, it is important to report the difficulty to the appropriate person as soon as possible, and to negotiate assistance where possible.

- Time management is a combination of effective work planning and control of time (eg through delegation and assertiveness).

- Legal and policy constraints apply to your working practices in areas such as maintaining your own work area and respecting confidentiality. (Recap your learning from Chapter 2 if you need to.)

Keywords

- **Action plan:** detailed record of all the tasks involved in a complex project – normally including start and finish dates and responsibility for each task

- **Deadline:** a set time when a task must be completed

- **Job description:** a written summary of the main duties and tasks required as part of a particular job

- **Important tasks:** tasks which affect other people or outcomes; on which others depend; or which have significant (positive or negative) impact

- **Planning aids:** tools, formats and techniques for organising tasks and projects

- **Planning schedule:** a form of a bar chart, but each division of space represents both an amount of time and an amount of work to be done in that time

- **Prioritising:** ordering tasks according to their degree of urgency and importance

- **Routine tasks:** the general daily, weekly, monthly tasks which make up a job

- **Schedule:** the allocation of tasks to appropriate times/dates when they will be tackled or completed

- **Time management:** ensuring that work is carried out efficiently and effectively, so that all tasks are completed on time and within the time available

- **Urgent tasks:** tasks for which there is a deadline in the near future

1 **For each of the following tasks, select their priority category from the picklist.**

Task	Category	
Preparing a petty cash summary by the end of next week		▼
Packing up out of date files to be archived		▼
Preparing a report for a meeting tomorrow		▼
Replenishing the milk in the kitchen this morning		▼

Picklist:

Not urgent but important
Not urgent or important
Urgent but not important
Urgent and important

2 **Complete the missing terms using the picklist below.**

A(n) [_____ ▼] is a simple short-term planning tool and consists of a checklist listing the tasks that need completing for a particular day.

A(n) [_____ ▼] [_____] is a detailed planning tool which can be used for complex longer-term projects.

Picklist for line items:

action plan
To Do list

3 You have been asked to prepare a report for your manager which must be with her on Wednesday 22 August. You will need to requisition some files for this, which will take a day to arrive. You estimate that the research will take you three days and the analysis required another two days. The report will be with the typist for a further day and then you will need one final day for checking and proofing.

The latest date on which you could start work on this report is [_____]

4 You are due to complete the weekly supplier payment run, to be given to your manager for review and authorisation by 4pm on Thursday. However, due to an unexpected fire drill, you have been delayed by an hour. **Which course of action would be best?**

Action	✓
Carry on with the work, until completed at 5pm	
Report the delay to your manager	
Go home early without completing the payment run	
Start on one of tomorrow's tasks, and complete the payment run later	

5   Your company's working procedures say that supplier payment runs must be reviewed and authorised by the purchases ledger manager, and then the BACS payment request should be signed by two directors.

Because the payment run was completed late, you decide to give it immediately to one of the directors to sign the BACS payment request, and then send it to the bank.

Which THREE consequences from the list below are likely as a result of this situation?

Consequences	✓
A supplier is paid and the manager knows there are queries on the account.	
The bank rejects the BACS payment request for lack of signatures.	
The bank rejects the BACS payment request as it has not been authorised by the purchases ledger manager.	
Suppliers' payments are delayed, due to bank rejection.	

Working as part of a team

Learning outcomes

2.2	Identify the features of an effective finance team
	• Know the characteristics of an effective team: good communication channels, shared values, a mix of complementary skills, clear leadership, common purpose and clearly defined roles and responsibilities
	• Know the skills, competencies and behaviours required of individuals within a high-performing team: trust, shared goals and values, clear roles and responsibilities, effective communication, numeracy skills, clear leadership, every member feels valued, a mix of complementary skills and diversity
	• Know the actions a team member can take to support the success of the finance team: work independently but aware of the work of others, help others in the team wherever possible, take responsibility for completing work within targets and to standard, communicate effectively, contribute ideas, understand within the team, understand individual and team objectives, have commitment to achieving team and individual objectives.
3.3	Plan workload to meet the needs of the organisation
	• Understand the impact on others of not completing specified tasks.

Assessment context

Working as part of a team is a significant part of the unit syllabus, and is likely to be examined. The assessment may require you to assess the impact on others of not completing tasks, appropriate actions to take when there are conflicting deadlines, and the qualities of good teamwork.

Qualification context

Some of the themes of this chapter, such as meeting deadlines, will overlap with the chapter on 'Working independently'.

The themes in this chapter may be referred to generally, in other units at all levels, but not examined specifically.

Business context

Being able to work as part of a team is an essential part of the finance role in most organisations. Good teamwork will maximise efficiency and increase creativity, quality and motivation, as well as leading to the achievement of common goals. Research has shown that teams can achieve work more quickly and effectively than people taking on a project on their own.

Chapter overview

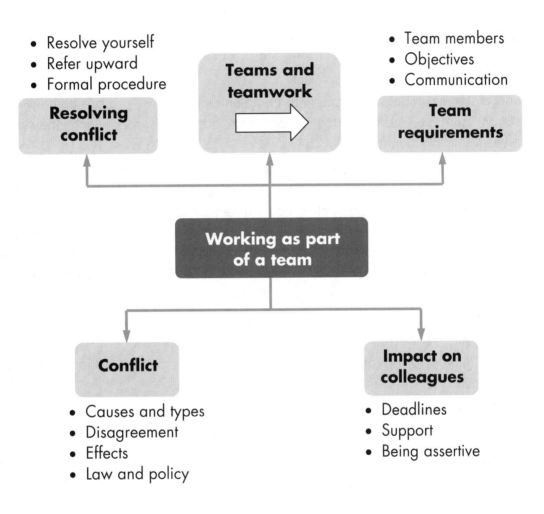

- Resolve yourself
- Refer upward
- Formal procedure

Resolving conflict

Teams and teamwork

- Team members
- Objectives
- Communication

Team requirements

Working as part of a team

Conflict

- Causes and types
- Disagreement
- Effects
- Law and policy

Impact on colleagues

- Deadlines
- Support
- Being assertive

Introduction

Our previous chapter covered techniques that can be helpful when working independently. This chapter looks at the working environment from a different perspective, and this is when not working alone, but as a team member.

1 Teams and team working

In most work situations, you will find that you are not working in isolation, but as part of a work group. This work group might be a department such as the Accounts department, or a section of a department such as the Payroll section. If this group works closely together, and has a strong sense of shared goals and identity, it may be thought of as a **team**.

A team is a small number of people with complementary skills who are committed to a common purpose, performance goals and approach, for which they hold themselves jointly accountable.

People working together in organisations need to recognise their mutual obligations to each other, and their shared tasks and objectives. They need to recognise their roles and relationships with respect to each other, as determined by their position and function in the team and in the organisation. They need to treat each other with mutual respect, within guidelines of acceptable and professional behaviour. They need to resolve any differences and conflicts that may reduce personal and team effectiveness. That's what team working is all about.

1.1 Advantages of team working

There are a number of advantages to working as part of a team rather than on an individual basis.

- **Additional resources**: a team provides extra skills, information, ideas and work hours, compared with working on your own.

- **Inspiration**: teams are particularly useful for generating ideas and solving problems, because different people's ideas and viewpoints can influence the work and thinking of others.

- **Motivation**: the shared efforts of a team and the help and support of its members can often provide additional motivation and satisfaction to team members in their work.

- **Communication**: team working is a great way to get people talking about how their tasks depend on each other, and how they can work together to solve problems. Teams are a key tool for **co-ordination** in organisations, especially where team members (for a project, say) are drawn from different functions or units, so that there is plenty of lateral or cross-functional communication.

- **Synergy**: for all the above reasons, teams can often accomplish more than the same individuals working alone. The concept of synergy describes how sometimes two heads are not just better than one: they are better than two! When people work together effectively, 2 + 2 = 5.

1.2 The downside of team working

Team working is often not easy! Individuals have different skills, personalities and working styles and, although this can contribute to team ideas and decisions, it can also cause frictions and conflicts within the team. Conflicts and disagreements (as we see later) can get in the way of effective team performance.

Some other disadvantages of team working are that decision making takes longer (because of the need to take different views into account) and the process of working together and maintaining good relationships can actually distract team members from the task at hand.

2 Working as part of a team

Effective team working requires a number of elements:

- A mix and balance of people in the team
- Clear shared objectives and performance feedback
- Co-ordination, collaboration and communication

2.1 Team members

In order for a team to function well together, and to fulfil its task objectives, it needs to have a mix and balance of:

- Required skills, experience and knowledge, which people can contribute to the task. Different people will have varying strengths and weaknesses: team working helps to even this out – and fill any gaps!

- The way people contribute to the functioning of the team. These are sometimes called 'team roles'. Some members will be leaders; some 'ideas' people; others will be better at implementing or following through the ideas; still others will be the ones who help team discussion along and act as peacemakers if there is **conflict**. All these roles are needed in a well-functioning team.

Key term

Conflicts are the opposing forces or interests, causing disagreement, competition or hostility.

It is important for you to identify your own role in the team's performance and maintenance. What does the team need you to do, competently and reliably, in order to achieve its objectives? What does the team need you to contribute, in order to maintain effective team working?

Do not underestimate the importance of small contributions to good working relationships, like replenishing the biscuit tin, or offering support to a colleague. Conversely, do not underestimate the negative effect on team working of letting conflicts fester, failing to 'pull your weight' in the team, or failing to honour your commitments to other team members.

2.2 Objectives and feedback

In order for a team to work well, it must have a well-defined and well-understood purpose and objectives, which apply to all its members. This ensures that all members are working towards the same goals. Each member should have clearly set out (or jointly agreed) responsibilities – but essentially, the focus is less on individual achievement than on contributing to group achievement.

In some cases, the objectives of a team will be set for it by the nature of its work, and the team leader's goals for how the work should be carried out.

However, where a new team has been set up for a task or project, it may be necessary to negotiate and jointly agree objectives, targets and standards for the team.

The team will require regular feedback: information on its progress and results, so that it can learn, correct or adjust its performance – or celebrate its successes.

Let's consider the Accounts department as an example of a team with objectives. The Accounts department will have the standing objective of preparing monthly cost accounts and annual financial accounts, invoicing and receiving money from customers, paying suppliers and other expenses – and so on. There are also likely to be specific targets and standards for how quickly, efficiently and accurately these tasks are carried out – which can be used for performance measurement and management.

2.3 Collaboration, co-ordination and communication

Team working is about collaboration (working together) and co-ordination (making sure that each member's work 'fits' with the work of others and contributes to the team's objectives). The key point is that the work that you do impacts upon the work of other people: positively or negatively!

Information that you provide will be used by other members of the team. They may not be able to complete their tasks until you have completed yours. Therefore, schedules and working methods must be set by the team leader – or by **negotiation** among the group – to ensure that the work of all members is co-ordinated and integrated.

As we saw in Chapter 5, it is always important to meet deadlines and commitments: within a team, it is even more important that each individual fulfils their responsibilities, according to agreed schedules and working practices, in order for the team to achieve its objectives.

If any team member anticipates trouble meeting their commitments, they must inform the team leader and affected colleagues, and work with them to devise options to resolve the situation.

In general, the more communication between team members – and between the team and its leader – the more effective the team's performance will be. Among other things, this means that conflicts between team members must be resolved, so that they don't interfere with communication.

Illustration 1: Collaboration

A few months into your time at Southfield Electronics, you are asked by Jenny Faulkner, the Financial Accountant, to form a small project team with Amy Laval (Accounts Clerk), Sam Piper (the new Accounts Clerk), Kellie McDonald (Assistant Financial Accountant) and John Yeo (Sales Manager).

This morning, Friday 3 March, you, Amy, Sam, Kellie and John had a meeting with Jenny to discuss the purpose of the project team and the work that is to be done.

Jenny explained that the company is looking into changing its credit terms to credit customers and, in particular, is reviewing its policy of offering prompt payment discounts to some customers. This will require a wide-ranging analysis of credit sales, and the payment patterns of all credit customers, in order to forecast the effect of the change of policy on sales. Jenny handed out the following briefing notes.

CREDIT SALES PROJECT: BRIEFING NOTES

OBJECTIVE

Analysis of credit limits and payment patterns of all credit customers – to be produced by Kellie McDonald by Friday 31 March.

TASKS

Accounts clerks to analyse each credit customer's account for the last year. Analysis to be prepared as follows:

- Credit limit
- Number of times credit limit exceeded
- Average amount by which credit limit exceeded
- Total credit sales for the year
- If prompt payment discount offered, percentage of total credit sales on which discount is taken
- Monthly average of outstanding amount which has been due for more than 60 days and more than 90 days

[Your Name] – credit customers from A to G
Amy Laval – credit customers from H to N
Sam Piper – credit customers from O to Z

[Your Name] is also to set up a computer spreadsheet for the analysed data. Amy Laval and Sam Piper are to input the data to the spreadsheet. Kellie McDonald is to write the final report summarising the findings regarding credit limits and payment patterns, with comments on key findings by John Yeo, where relevant.

RESOURCES

Computerised receivables ledger
Monthly aged receivables listing
Manual customer data file

TIMETABLE

Computer spreadsheet to be completed by Friday 10 March
Accounts assistants' analysis to be completed by Monday 20 March
Completed spreadsheet to Kellie McDonald by Friday 24 March

You realise that, given your existing workload, you cannot possibly set up the spreadsheet and analyse all of your assigned credit customers by the due dates. You voice this concern to Jenny, and explain that you will also need test data to be input into the spreadsheet.

Jenny agrees that perhaps this is asking too much and assigns customers beginning with E and F to Amy and customers beginning with G to Sam, leaving you with a more manageable workload. Jenny also decides that Sam should have the analysis for 30 credit customers ready for you to input as test data on 13 March.

Kellie agrees to supervise the analysis and sets up a weekly meeting every Friday morning at 10:00am in order to assess the team's progress.

3 The impact of your work on colleagues

Members of an accounting section are generally interdependent: their work objectives and outputs are often linked to each other. This is even more evident in fully team-based activities and projects, where tasks, or components or stages of tasks, are shared among team members. The outputs of one person's activity will become the inputs to another's.

The most important aspect of this is that if one team member fails to complete their allotted/agreed tasks, or fails to complete them on time, there will be an impact on other team members and their work.

Activity 1: Not meeting deadlines

From the learning you have already completed in the previous chapter, on a separate page, explain three impacts on a team of one member failing to meet an agreed deadline for project work.

3.1 Deadlines

We covered the importance of meeting departmental deadlines, and what to do if you encounter problems in meeting deadlines, in Chapter 5. There, we were looking at deadlines faced when working independently – but we emphasised that your work is almost always intended for use by someone else, who may rely on its timely completion. The same thing applies in team working – only more so, because of the need to co-ordinate the work of more than one person.

Refresh your memory about the importance of meeting deadlines, and what to do if you encounter problems, if you need to, by re-reading the relevant section of Chapter 5.

3.2 Mutual assistance and support

There will undoubtedly be occasions when a team member realises that they cannot fulfil a work commitment, because the schedule turns out to be unrealistic, or because unforeseen factors have created a lack of time or resources.

On such occasions, other members of the team should be prepared to provide assistance or support, as required. For example, if one team member is running out of time to carry out a task, another could offer to help (if they have extra time available) or could allow the person struggling to have first option on equipment time, say. Provided that it does not impact negatively on your own work, or become a recurring pattern, 'doing a colleague a favour' can contribute to good working relationships and team performance.

In some cases, support will be personal as well as practical. Team members may support each other when they are struggling, through empathetic listening, collaborative problem solving, encouragement, constructive feedback and so on.

Illustration 2: Progress meeting

Let's return to the Southfield Electronics credit sales project. On 10 March at 10:00am, the first project progress meeting is held. You report that you have the spreadsheet set up and are ready for the test data to be input on Monday. Kellie checks with Sam to ensure that the test data will be ready by Monday morning. Unfortunately, Sam has to admit that he is struggling with the analysis so far and has only analysed data for 18 customers: he asks for assistance. Kellie asks you and Amy about your workloads.

You feel that you have to get on with your analysis of credit customers, as your time has been taken up by the spreadsheet. Amy also feels that, in order to meet the deadline of 20 March for her analysis, she has no spare time. However, as Amy has already completed analyses of 29 customers, she suggests that the remaining 12 analyses required for the test data are simply taken from her customers. Kellie agrees and it is further agreed that you will input the test data on Monday as originally planned.

Activity 2: Assistance and support

On Monday 22 March 20X0, you are asked to take part in a team project that will take about one month – as well as your normal tasks for the financial accounts section. The team is to provide detailed costings for a new line of children's toys. It is made up of three accounts assistants (including you), a senior accounts assistant and the team leader (the cost accountant). The costings must be ready for the monthly board meeting on Wednesday 21 April.

On Tuesday 6 April, at the weekly project team meeting, one of the other accounts assistants timidly admits that she had forgotten that the following weekend was the Easter holiday: she will not be able to meet her stage deadline. She believes that she can analyse the figures by the next day, but will not have time to input them to the computer on Thursday, the last working day of the week.

You know that you are likely to have some spare time on Thursday, as you are ahead with your routine tasks and have already completed your project tasks. However, you do not expect to have any spare time before Thursday.

What should you do in this situation? Tick the correct box.

Offer to help input the figures on Thursday ☐

Ask the other accounts assistant to complete the work in her own time outside of work ☐

Offer to help analyse the figures on Wednesday ☐

Do nothing as it is not really your problem ☐

3.3 Being appropriately assertive

As we mentioned in Chapter 5, it is important to protect your time and scheduled priorities – in order to avoid having them disrupted by the demands of other team members.

Your ability to do this, and what course of action is appropriate in a given situation, depends on a number of factors. You will need to consider:

- The authority of the person making an unexpected demand on your time. Does this person have the 'right' to ask you?

- The nature of the request: is it appropriate and reasonable, and in the best interests of the effectiveness and efficiency of the department – or can you propose a better course of action?

- The impact on other people and tasks, if you go ahead with the demand: for example, will it prevent you from meeting other deadlines?

- Which of the people making conflicting demands on you has the most authority? If they have equal authority, you might be able to ask them to negotiate a compromise between them – or you may have to refer the matter upwards to a higher authority for a decision.

- What is the most courteous, respectful, professional and assertive way to resolve the problem – without inappropriately sacrificing your own needs and interests?

Assertive communication means standing up for your own rights, needs and opinions (ie not being passive or a 'doormat') – without dismissing the rights, needs or opinions of others (ie not being 'aggressive').

You have a right to say 'no' to inappropriate or unreasonable demands – but you can choose to do this in a way that is calm, courteous, professional, positive and co-operative. The key is to state clearly and directly what the problem is, and what you want or do not want to happen. If possible, explain why you cannot comply with a demand because of its impact on your work or the interests of the team: this should defuse any suspicion that you are just being 'selfish'! You might then be able to propose alternative solutions to meet the other person's needs (can you perform their task later, or get the assistance you need to fit it in, or propose someone better placed to do it than you?) – or invite them to make alternative suggestions, which you will consider positively.

Illustration 3: Request and response

Back at the Southfield Electronics credit sales project, it is now the end of the day on Wednesday 22 March. You are finalising the spreadsheets for Kellie McDonald, ready to submit them to her, as requested, on Friday.

Just as you are packing up for the day, Ron Howard, another of the Assistant Financial Accountants to whom you report, comes and asks you to do a task for him first thing tomorrow. He estimates it will take you about half a day – and it will enable him to take the morning off to take his wife to the doctor.

You are aware that you do not have half a day to spare, if you are to complete your spreadsheet work for the project. So you say calmly and courteously to Ron:

'I'm sorry, Ron, but I have an important deadline coming up on the credit sales project. I simply don't have any time to spare tomorrow. I would love to be able to help you out – but if I don't get the spreadsheet done, Kellie and John Yeo will not have time to work on their final report.'

Ron says loudly that his work should take equal priority to Kellie's – particularly since it is genuine Accounts department work, 'not some project thing'. Obviously, you cannot take this view, since you have agreed your schedule with Kellie, who has equal authority to Ron – and also the backing of Jenny Faulkner.

Without backing down, you continue to calmly offer constructive options, suggesting that if Ron were to speak to Kellie and explain the situation, she might be able to stretch your project deadline a little – or one of the other accounts clerks might be able to help him.

Activity 3: Being assertive

Discuss how effectively you have handled the situation in the Illustration 3 scenario above. What are the key points of the argument you make for protecting your time in this scenario?

Activity 4: Assertive behaviour

Which of the following is the best description of assertive behaviour?

Dismissing the rights, needs or opinions of others ☐

Standing up for your own rights, needs and opinions ☐

4 Conflict and dissatisfaction at work

Conflict is the clash of opposing 'forces' – including the personalities, interests and attitudes of individuals and groups. In any working relationship or team, there are bound to be disagreements and conflicts of various kinds. There are also likely to be times when you are dissatisfied with something at work: for example, unresolved problems, frustrations, poor working conditions or unfair treatment.

Your aim in the workplace is to be able to handle disagreements, conflicts and dissatisfactions constructively, so that you can maintain good working relations and efficient individual and team working.

4.1 Causes and types of conflict

In any working relationship or team, there are bound to be conflicts on occasion. Such conflicts may be due to:

- Differences in personality (eg an outgoing person irritating a quiet, reflective person)

- Differences in working style (eg if one person likes to plan ahead and the other doesn't)

- Differences in status (eg if team members feel powerless or micro-managed by a powerful boss, or unable to raise problems because a manager is seen as 'unapproachable')

- The interdependency of work (eg if one person or team is frustrated by delays caused by another's missed deadline, or someone within the team isn't 'pulling their weight' and leaves others with more work to do)

- Competition between groups or departments for limited resources (including office space, finance, information, status and power). This is a major cause of conflict, whether we're talking about individuals or nations!

- Unfair treatment (eg a manager gives an unfairly harsh evaluation, or refuses legitimate requests for help)

- Hurtful treatment (eg a team member is bullying, offensive, sexist or racist)

Differences, frustrations and competition by themselves don't necessarily lead to conflict: they can even be positive forces, helping people to solve problems or to lift their performance. However, they can escalate or deteriorate into harmful conflict if there is a lack of communication and problem solving – or if work demands put pressure on people and situations.

4.2 Disagreement

It is important that you are able to disagree with someone – and still maintain good working relations! For example, suppose that your supervisor believes that one method of dealing with purchase invoices is the most efficient, but you have a different view. If you have tried to persuade your supervisor that your method is more efficient, but have failed to do so, you need to accept the superior authority, forget the argument and continue with your tasks. It is more important to be effective than to be right!

4.3 More serious conflicts

Other disagreements or conflicts may be more serious: someone may be disobeying agreed rules or procedures, say, or behaving in unacceptable or even illegal ways (eg in the case of sexual harassment, bullying or breaking safety rules).

You need to be aware of the limits of your authority to deal with such problems. You may be able to sort some out yourself (eg by having an honest talk with a colleague about how their behaviour affects you or the team). In some instances, however, you may need to take it to a higher authority: a process called **'escalation'**. We will consider a range of conflict resolution options below.

4.4 Effects of unresolved conflict and dissatisfaction

If conflict and dissatisfaction are allowed to go unresolved, or to get worse, they can have a negative impact on the functioning and effectiveness of the team.

- Individuals with unresolved dissatisfactions may become resentful, demotivated and uncooperative. They may withdraw their contribution to the group – or actively seek to sabotage it.

- The cause of the dissatisfaction may itself be a barrier to effective performance (eg lack of resources).

- Unresolved conflict between individuals can result in reduced communication, co-ordination and co-operation between them.

- Conflict between individuals may split the team into 'factions', escalating rivalry and hostility within the team.

- Conflict can polarise differing viewpoints, causing people to hold extreme views, and to dig their heels in, in disagreements. This may make it impossible to 'agree to disagree' – and create unbalanced and risky decisions.

In other words, unresolved conflict can significantly interfere with team working! On the other hand, the effective management of conflict and dissatisfaction can contribute to better teamwork – and to more productive working relationships.

4.5 Law and policy frameworks for positive working relations

Major legislation in the UK and EU is directed at preventing harassment and discrimination against people at work due to their sex or sexual orientation, race or ethnicity, religion, age or disability. This is broadly called 'equal opportunity' law.

Employers must not discriminate in giving people access to jobs, promotion, training or benefits, and you may have rights as a job applicant or employee in these areas. However, employees are also required not to 'harass' others in the workplace by using language or behaviour which intimidates, denigrates or offends.

It is said that 'the law is a floor': it only sets minimum standards of acceptable behaviour. Organisational policies and practices (together with professional codes of conduct) may go beyond basic non-discrimination, to try to foster positive values for working relationships, such as courtesy, respect, professionalism and teamwork.

5 Resolving conflicts and dissatisfactions

5.1 Dealing with dissatisfactions

Some dissatisfactions at work may be within your competence and authority to resolve yourself, or by informal negotiation with your supervisor or colleagues. If your workload is too heavy, for example, you may be able to adjust your schedule or work plans, or ask a colleague to help you. If you get headaches from inadequate light at your desk, you may be able to reposition your desk, or requisition a desk lamp, or ask colleagues' permission to keep window blinds open.

Some dissatisfactions, however, may be beyond your competence or authority to resolve yourself. In such cases, you may need to take the problem first to your immediate supervisor or line manager, who may be able to propose or mobilise solutions to the problem.

You may be advised to refer the problem to another appropriate person. If your dissatisfaction is with poor training, for example, you may be advised to approach the training or HR manager. If you are frustrated by the performance of the office cleaners, you might be advised to communicate with the office manager.

5.2 Conflicts you can resolve yourself

Conflicts can be managed informally in several ways.

- If you have a problem working with someone, you might initially attempt direct, informal discussion with the person concerned. Where there is a personality or style clash, this gets the problem out in the open and gives an opportunity to clear up any misunderstandings.

- Problems of incompatible working styles or excessive work demands are matters which can be taken to your supervisor, who will be able to help you develop solutions to the problem.

- If your conflict is with someone in authority over you, you may have to discuss the matter with someone higher up in the organisation. This is probably best handled using more formal channels, called 'grievance procedures' – discussed later.

Where the interests or styles of different parties are genuinely incompatible, you may need to work together to explore a range of options that will at least partially satisfy both parties. This is a process called negotiation. You may have to give or concede something the other party wants in return for getting something that you want: a process of bargaining, which often results in a mutually acceptable compromise.

However, the best approach – most satisfying for both parties **and** most likely to preserve positive relationships – is to attempt to find a mutually satisfying or 'win–win' solution. The 'win–win' model states that there are three basic ways in which a conflict or problem can be worked out:

- One party gets what they want at the expense of the other: 'win–lose'. For example, if two parties are fighting over an orange, one gets the orange, and the other gets nothing. However well justified the solution, there is often lingering resentment on the part of the 'losing' party.

- A compromise solution is found, so that neither party gets what they really wanted: 'lose–lose'. For example: both parties get half an orange each. However 'logical' such a solution is, there is often lingering dissatisfaction on both sides.

- Both parties work together to understand each other's needs and concerns, and generate options to try to get as close as possible to what each party really wants: 'win–win'. A 'win–win' result may not be possible but, in the process of working together and trying to get the best outcome for both sides, new options may be created – and co-operation will be enhanced. So, for example, it may come out in discussion that one party likes orange juice, while another wants the zest of the orange to make a cake: there is now a way of dividing up the orange that leaves both parties satisfied!

Activity 5: Conflict resolution

Two of your team members are arguing over who gets to use the desk by the window.

Of the following options, which is the only one that may result in a 'win–win' situation?

The team members get the window desk on alternate days or weeks. ☐

Find out why each wants the window desk and look for solutions to
meet their needs. ☐

One team member gets the window desk, the other doesn't. ☐

If personality clash is the main source of conflict, you may have to arrange (or request) a way of working with the other person as little as possible. If the problems persist, you may need to refer them upwards: to have your supervisor (or another appropriate third party) mediate – or arrange for you to work in different areas or teams.

5.3 Referring conflicts upwards

In many cases, conflicts and dissatisfactions can be dealt with by the individuals involved. In other cases, however, they may be beyond your authority or ability to resolve, and may require escalation.

It may be necessary to report the incident or conflict to a more senior person for help in handling it. Your supervisor or manager may be able to make decisions to resolve the matter (eg by reallocating resources or changing schedules), or may be in a position to enforce rules and procedures – or may simply be more persuasive getting a point across than you are!

In the first instance, you should go to your supervisor – or whoever has authority over both parties in the conflict. For a conflict within a project team, for example, you might talk to the team leader.

If your conflict is with your own supervisor or line manager, the problem may have to be escalated 'up the line' to their immediate manager. Obviously, you will have to think carefully about whether and how you do this. Is the issue serious enough to risk damaging your working relationship with your boss? Do you have a strong, reasonable 'case', supported by evidence, for any allegations you feel you need to make? Can the issue be put in a positive light, with the aim of co-operative problem solving, in the interest of improving working relationships and work performance?

Illustration 4: Response to conflict

Back at Southfield Electronics, Ron did not take well your courteous refusal to take on extra work at short notice. He shouted at you and stormed out of the office. The following day, when he came in late, he was rude to you, and blamed you loudly for his being behind on his work. He says that your 'uncooperative behaviour' will be reflected on your performance appraisal.

What should you do?

You calmly but assertively explain to Ron that you did in fact attempt to be as helpful as possible, but that you had prior work commitments that could not be broken. You refer him, once again, to Kellie McDonald, so that they can resolve the 'time-sharing' issue between them.

If Ron continues to be aggressive and hostile in his manner towards you, you will seek a confidential meeting with Jenny Faulkner (the Financial Accountant) to explain the situation to her.

Jenny may be able to meet with Kellie and Ron (to resolve the issue of how your time is allocated) and perhaps with you and Ron (to resolve the conflict between you). She will be able to discipline Ron, if necessary, for his inappropriate behaviour.

5.4 Formal grievance procedures

In some cases, the matter may be so serious that a more formal approach needs to be adopted.

A **grievance** is a formal complaint by an individual who feels that they are being wrongly or unfairly treated by a colleague or manager at work. Such complaints may include:

- Harassment or bullying
- Unfair or discriminatory treatment by managers due to race, gender or disability
- An employee being given an unfair workload
- An employee being unfairly blocked for promotion

All organisations should have a written **grievance procedure** which is communicated to all employees. This should state to whom an employee should go with a particular type of grievance. It will often be their line manager. If the grievance is against the line manager, or if it cannot be sorted out at that level, a more senior manager will be consulted, and the HR department may become involved.

If the grievance cannot be sorted out internally, the employee may have to take the problem before an Employment Tribunal, which works as an independent informal court.

Assessment focus point

For this topic you may be assessed by being given a specific task which has not been completed, and asked to state the impact on others within a team.

The assessment may also ask you about the characteristics of a high performing team, either in a theoretical way or as a practical scenario-based task.

Finally, the subject of dissatisfaction may be assessed using a scenario, and asking you to identify the issue or resolve it.

As in other tasks, reading the information presented completely and carefully is important.

Chapter summary

- Team working, as opposed to working individually, can provide additional resources, inspiration, motivation and communication (for co-ordination).

- When a team is set up, it is important to establish a mix and balance of members; shared, appropriate resources; and agreed working methods, timescales and schedules.

- It may be necessary to provide assistance or support to other team members from time to time, in order to achieve the objectives of the team.

- There will often be conflicts in working relationships, which may be caused by differences in personality, working style or status, or work demands.

- In general, disagreements or conflicts should be dealt with in such a way as to maintain relations and relationships. This requires positive, assertive communication.

- In some cases, conflicts can be satisfactorily dealt with between individuals, but in more serious cases an employee may have to report a matter to a line manager with the authority to resolve matters or enforce rules.

- Employers should have a written grievance procedure policy which employees can follow if the grievance needs to be properly investigated and arbitrated by senior management.

Keywords

- **Assertive communication:** A style of communication based on respecting your own rights – without trampling on the rights of others

- **Conflict:** Opposing forces or interests, causing disagreement, competition or hostility

- **Co-ordination:** The process by which the work of different individuals and teams is linked together to achieve shared objectives

- **Escalation:** Taking a problem to a higher level of management for resolution

- **Grievance:** A complaint brought by an employee who feels wrongly treated by colleagues or managers

- **Grievance procedure:** An employer's formalised procedure for investigating and resolving a grievance

- **Negotiation:** A process of bargaining to reach a solution in a situation where there is a conflict of interests

- **Synergy:** A process in team working by which 'the whole is greater than the sum of its parts' – or 2 + 2 = 5

- **Team:** A group of employees working together to meet shared objectives

Test your learning

1   **Which two of the following might be teams operating within an accounting function? Tick the correct boxes.**

	✓
Human resources team	
Inventory control section	
Payroll section	
Receivables ledger team	

2   **Give examples of roles that people might occupy in a well-balanced team.**

3   **If a team is working to complete a particular project, why is it important that all schedules and timetables are (a) agreed and (b) met?**

4   **Explain how mutual assistance within a team can provide synergies.**

5   You have recently joined the Accounting department of a company and have found one of your fellow accounts assistants to be extremely rude to you and constantly demanding that you fetch the coffee, clean up the kitchen etc.

   Which of the following would be the best course of action in the first instance?

	✓
Complain to your line manager	
Discuss your concerns with your colleague	
Do nothing	
Resign from your position	

6   You and a colleague both need access to the same file at the same time. You both need it to compile reports for your managers, for the following morning. It is now 3:00pm and each of you will need it for two hours to do this work. **Suggest (a) a win–lose, (b) a compromise and (c) a win–win solution in the scenario. What result can you foresee from each solution?**

7 **Which of the following would be examples of possible 'grievances' in the workplace? Tick the correct boxes.**

	✓
An argument with a fellow employee over the tidiness of their work space	☐
An employee being given an unfair workload	☐
An employee being blocked for promotion	☐
Having to share a printer with another department	☐
Sexual or racial harassment	☐
Unfair treatment or discrimination due to race, gender or disability	☐

Developing skills and knowledge

7

Learning outcomes

2.3	Identify development needs
	• Know the importance of continuing professional development (CPD) to finance staff
	• Be able to review own performance and use feedback from others
	• Be able to identify development objectives and activities to address objectives

Assessment context

CPD is one of the important elements of the unit syllabus, and is very likely to be examined. An example of assessment tasks may present a scenario where training is needed and require that relevant activities are chosen, and with relevant timescales for completion. The task may also require that benefits and reasons for CPD are explained.

Qualification context

This chapter focuses on the developing of skills and knowledge for accountants. It is not directly linked to any of the other topics in this unit, except that further knowledge of them, eg communication skills, may be considered to be useful CPD. It is also not directly linked to any of the other units at this level. Reference to CPD may be made occasionally in other units in Levels 3 and 4.

Business context

Maintaining and developing knowledge and skills that are relevant to the job is of benefit to both employers and the individuals involved. Employers may support provision of CPD as they benefit by having knowledgeable staff, who can work efficiently, and meet current standards.

Chapter overview

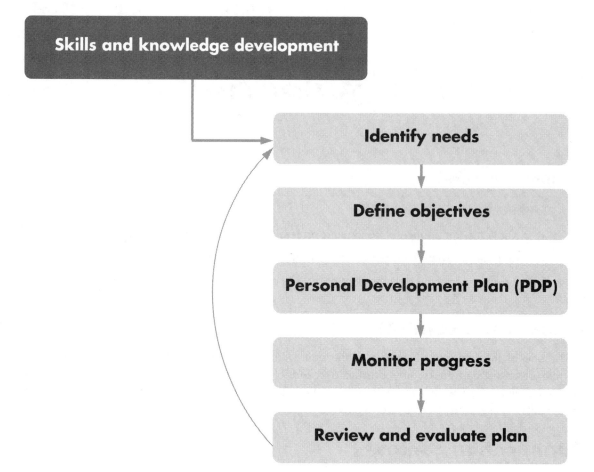

Skills and knowledge development

Identify needs

Define objectives

Personal Development Plan (PDP)

Monitor progress

Review and evaluate plan

Introduction

This chapter explains why finance professionals must keep their knowledge, and skills up to date. We also look at how this can be achieved through a process of on-going training, and continuous professional development.

1 Continuing Professional Development

Let's start with some useful definitions.

- **Training** is a process of using learning experiences to achieve more effective performance in particular work activities or roles.

- **Development** is a broader process of growth in knowledge and capabilities. In addition to education and training, individuals may be encouraged to gain experience of different roles in an organisation, and increasing challenges (perhaps through promotion within the organisation, or 'career development').

- **Continuing Professional Development** (CPD) is a systematic process of planning for the future and of gaining experience and training relevant to the directions in which employees want to develop – both within the current job role and in future career progression.

Members of professional bodies (such as the AAT, ACCA or ICAEW) are required to complete a certain amount of CPD as a condition of continuing membership. This ensures that their knowledge and skills are always up to date and of a good standard. This, in turn, protects the interests of their clients and employers, as well as the standing and credibility of the professional bodies and the accounting profession.

As we will see, CPD can be pursued in a number of different ways. Individuals may undertake vocational training through the NVQ framework, or further education through universities and colleges. They may study for progression to membership of a professional body (like the AAT). They may receive instruction, training or coaching in the workplace. Or they may plan for self-development by a continual process of identifying their weaknesses, seeking opportunities to practise, gathering feedback, and learning from their mistakes.

A key feature of the CPD approach is that the responsibility for development lies mainly with the individual, in collaboration with their employers, and other parties such as the professional bodies.

You are responsible for maintaining CPD appropriate to:

- Your current job role: helping you to meet the requirements of the role better – and ensuring that you stay up to date with the changing requirements of the role, and/or changing developments in your field

- Your career aspirations: equipping yourself with the knowledge and skills you will require for higher-level roles, and enabling you to seek more challenging job opportunities.

1.1 Why is training and development important?

Training can represent a significant cost to a business – in terms of training costs (training providers and resources), staff time spent in training, and resulting lost production, or the costs of covering training absences with replacement staff or overtime working.

It is, therefore, important to be able to justify training effort and expenditure on the basis of sound business benefits!

The ongoing development of skills and knowledge has significant benefits for the learners/trainees themselves, and for the organisation in which they work.

Benefits for the individual	Benefits for the employing organisation
Greater confidence and flexibility	More competent job performance
Improved job performance (perhaps leading to increased rewards and recognition)	Competent performance achieved more quickly by new recruits
Greater job security	Less supervision required
Ability to take on more challenge and responsibility in the job	Increased efficiency and productivity, through faster, more skilled work
Increased prospects of promotion	Reduced cost of errors, reduced non-compliance with regulations/laws
Enhanced skills, which can be used outside the job (eg communication skills)	Supports employee initiative, ideas, flexibility and innovation
Satisfaction from greater contribution	Improved staff motivation and morale
Greater 'employability' and value in the job market	Enhanced ability to recruit and retain high-quality employees

Activity 1: CPD benefits

You have recently prepared, and agreed with your supervisor (Mrs Hoff), an Action Plan, showing targets and activities for your learning over the next six months. Having submitted this plan to the HR Manager (Mr Bolt), you receive the following email.

EMAIL	
From:	a.bolt@reeves.co.uk
To:	y.name@reeves.co.uk; g.hoff@reeves.co.uk
Date:	[Today's date]
Re:	Action Plan
Thank you for submitting Your Name's Action Plan for the next six months.	

I am somewhat concerned at the cost of such plans for the Accounts department as a whole. Every member of the department has submitted requests for training – and also for 'professional development' activity which does not seem to be directly related to their current job roles.

I am not sure that this can be justified, and will have to review the Action Plans and training requests in this light.

Required

Mrs Hoff asks you to email Mr Bolt in reply, explaining the importance and benefits of Continuing Professional Development.

2 Identifying your development needs

Learning needs and **career goals** are highly specific to each individual – and to particular work contexts and roles. Obviously, we can't tell you what your career aspirations are (or should be), what your strengths and weaknesses are, or what areas of knowledge or skill you may need to develop further. What we can do is to give you the tools to work these things out for yourself – whether in your workplace or in your assessment.

2.1 Identifying learning needs in your current job

The most obvious starting point for identifying learning needs may be: how well do I fulfil the requirements of my current work role?

To answer this question, you can simply think through what it is that you do on a day to day basis, or consider feedback you have received from your supervisor or line manager about your performance. You may receive more formal feedback reports, setting out recommendations for learning and development, from performance reviews or appraisals.

For a systematic 'start from scratch' analysis, you might start with two key documents used by organisations to define the requirements of a job and of a job-holder.

- Your **job description** or role description, which sets out what a person in your job should be able to do. It describes the requirements of the job.

- The **person specification** for your role, which sets out what sort of personal qualities the organisation is looking for in your role. It describes the requirements of the job-holder.

Having got to grips with what is required of you in your job, you can ask yourself some questions: do I have the knowledge and skills necessary to perform my tasks competently? What tasks in my job description am I not yet able to perform well? What desirable attributes in the person specification for my role do I currently lack? Putting this all together: what are my strengths and weaknesses in this role?

Illustration 1: Job description

When you joined Southfield Electronics, you were shown the following documents relating to your job role.

	JOB DESCRIPTION
Job title:	Accounts Clerk, financial accounting
Location:	London office
Job summary:	General financial accounting duties
Key responsibilities:	Administrative support for the financial accounts section, including opening post and handling telephone and email enquiries
	Obtaining quotes from suppliers
	Preparing daily cheque listings, sales invoices, credit notes and monthly sales summaries (using computer spreadsheets)
	Monthly receivables ledger control account reconciliation
	Responsibility for petty cash in the cashier's absence
Reporting structure:	Financial Accountant | Assistant Financial Accountants (2) and Payroll Manager | Accounts Clerk
Hours:	9:00am to 5:30pm Monday to Friday 1 hour for lunch
Training:	Induction training will be provided Continuing Professional Development encouraged
Prepared by:	Head of HR
Date:	March 20X0

Person specification		
Criteria	**Essential**	**Desirable**
Qualifications	GCSE English Language (Grade A*–C) GCSE Mathematics (Grade A*–C)	Undertaking AAT qualification Word processing qualification Level 3 Spreadsheets
Experience	Basic computer use General office procedures	Previous accounts or clerical/administrative experience
Communication	Ability to communicate effectively in a range of situations Understanding of the importance of confidentiality	Familiarity with different communication formats
Team working	Ability to work flexibly in a team Understanding of deadlines	Previous experience of working in a team
Personal skills/ attributes	Personal integrity Attention to detail Ability to handle pressure	Ability to work without supervision when required

You now want to put together some ideas about your training needs, for your upcoming review. You decide to start with your current job performance. Is there room for improvement in the way you fulfil the requirements set out in the job description and person specification?

You make the following notes in your Personal Development Journal.

- **Do I have the knowledge and skills necessary to perform my tasks competently?**

   I still struggle with the monthly receivables ledger control account reconciliation, which I know takes me longer than it should. This is not helped by the fact that I am not confident about double entry bookkeeping. Whenever I have to prepare a computer spreadsheet, I have to ask one of the other accounts assistants for help, as I don't know how to do it on my own.

- **What tasks in my job description am I not yet able to perform well?**

   I should be responsible for petty cash when the cashier is absent, but I have never been asked to do this nor do I know how to.

- **What desirable attributes in the person specification for my role do I currently lack?**

  The holder of my role should ideally have a Level 3 qualification in Spreadsheets, and I have not yet attained this.

From these answers, you are able to draw up a list of your most immediate learning needs.

Learning needs to improve in my current job

- I would benefit from help from a senior colleague to show me how to perform the receivables ledger reconciliation more efficiently.

- I would benefit from studying a textbook on double entry bookkeeping – or perhaps a short bookkeeping course.

- I should plan to attend a computer spreadsheet course or get instruction from a colleague, with a view to working towards a Level 3 qualification.

- I should ask to spend some time with the cashier being shown how she deals with petty cash claims and, perhaps, perform the task a few times under her supervision.

Strengths and weaknesses analysis

A more general approach to identifying your learning needs would be to review the requirements of your role and your performance in the role, and then to ask, simply: what are my strengths and weaknesses in this role?

- Identified strengths are areas that you can build on. They may represent a foundation for further learning – or areas in which you are ready to ask for more challenge or responsibility.

- Identified weaknesses are areas that need attention in order to bring your competence or confidence up to the required level. They may represent your most immediate learning needs.

Illustration 2: Strengths and weaknesses

Continuing your learning needs planning at Southfield Electronics, you review your job description and person specification, and note the various requirements of your current role. How well are you fulfilling those requirements?

You reflect on your own performance, remembering particular incidents that have highlighted good and bad points: finishing your workload early so that you could help other members of the project team; mistakes you made in your double entry bookkeeping; having to ask for help with the computer spreadsheets, because you didn't feel confident about doing them on your own...

You note down the feedback you have received from others on your performance: your supervisor's praise for well-written reports and emails; a colleague's comment that the receivables ledger reconciliation is taking you longer than it should...

You look at the tasks in the job description that you are (and are not yet) performing well, and the attributes in the person specification that you do (and do not yet) possess.

You now have a list of good points and bad points, and you decide to pick the three most important of each to build or work on.

Strengths	Weaknesses
(1) Efficient workload management, prioritisation and flexibility to help others	(1) Lack of full competence in double entry bookkeeping and receivables ledger reconciliation
(2) Effective communication using emails and reports	(2) Lack of confidence in preparing computer spreadsheets: not yet attained Level 3 qualification
(3) Good ability to work without supervision and under pressure when required	(3) Lack of knowledge/experience of petty cash procedures

Now you can draw up a list of learning objectives which will:

(a) Build on your strengths: you will volunteer to act as secretary to your next project team, in order to develop your communication and workload management skills further

(b) Address your identified weaknesses: you will plan learning activities to improve your double entry bookkeeping, receivables ledger reconciliation, use of computer spreadsheets, and knowledge of petty cash procedures

Activity 2: Job role documents

Required

Complete the following sentences using the picklist below.

The ⬇️ for your role sets out what sort of personal qualities the organisation is looking for in your role.

The ⬇️ sets out what a person in your job should be able to do.

Picklist:

job description
person specification

2.2 Other tools for learning needs analysis

Some organisations carry out formal learning needs analysis, by testing employees' performance on areas listed in a job description or competence definition, say, or by discussing learning needs as part of their annual **performance appraisals**.

Other approaches include:

- Keeping a Personal Development Journal, in which you note down any incidents at work which indicate a learning need (eg having to ask for assistance, making a mistake or getting a complaint or negative feedback from a colleague). These are sometimes called 'critical incidents', as they highlight an underlying issue or need.

- Scanning the office notice board, intranet pages or staff magazines for advertised training courses and opportunities which strike you as relevant to your job.

- Gathering feedback or assessments from each training course you undertake, pointing you to 'areas for further improvement' or follow-up learning.

- Asking your supervisor or colleagues for feedback on areas of your performance: 'What do you think I need to learn about or do better?' (An excellent source of information, particularly about your interpersonal skills, or how you work with others!)

2.3 Identifying learning needs to fit your future career aspirations

Although you may be happy with your current job role, most people do have ambitions to develop their career, for personal satisfaction and growth – and for higher status and rewards. In order to identify future learning needs, you will need to consider where you are aiming to go – whether within your current organisation or elsewhere. What are your **career goals**?

> **Career goals** are your aims in terms of the jobs or jobs you aspire to in the future.

Key term

Ambition is a helpful motivator for personal development – but take care to be realistic in your goals. As a first-year accounts assistant, it may be realistic to aspire to become an accounts supervisor, but perhaps not to aspire to be Finance Director within two years! Factor in any learning, experience, maturing and trust-earning that may be required to get from where you are to where you want to get to.

It may help to talk informally to colleagues and those in more senior roles about how they got to their positions. It may also be useful to have a more formal conversation with your line manager or the Human Resources Manager, to determine the realistic career goals for you as an individual – and what support and opportunities may be available within the organisation.

Once you have identified some goals, you need to plan how to get from your current position to the job that you aspire to.

First, you need to ensure that you are carrying out your current role efficiently and effectively! Then you must consider the requirements of the job that you wish to have.

You may need to talk to your line manager or the Human Resources Manager in order to find out the details of the knowledge, skills and any qualifications that are required for this job. Once you are armed with this information, you can begin to set yourself realistic and specific development objectives – just as you would for your current job role.

3 Defining your development objectives

Even if your organisation supports you in training and development planning, it is important that you define your own development objectives, within the context of your own strengths, weaknesses and career goals.

Effective objectives (whether for knowledge and skills development or for career development) are **SMART**:

S   Specific
M   Measurable
A   Agreed
R   Realistic
T   Time-bounded

3.1 Specific

Specificity is necessary in order for a plan of action to be drawn up. 'To improve my use of spreadsheets soon' is far too vague to suggest an action plan – or to get you motivated! 'To complete a level 2 spreadsheet safety training course by October' is a much better guide to what (exactly) you want to do!

Try to be exact about what you hope to achieve or be able to do.

3.2 Measurable

You need to be able to review how you are progressing towards your goals – and whether you've reached them – so you need to state your objectives in a way that will enable you to measure or assess your performance.

How will you (or others) know how much progress you've made? How will you (or others) define completion or success? What test will you be able to pass? What will you be able to do that you couldn't do before? (Note that your Learning Outcomes for this unit are designed to be measurable in this way.)

Plan up front for when, how often and how your progress towards meeting the objective will be monitored and reviewed.

3.3 Agreed

In many cases the achievement of development objectives will require the commitment of resources from your employer: the loss of your time while you study or train, the costs of training, your manager's time coaching you and so on. Therefore, it is important that any personal development objectives are agreed with your supervisor or line manager. (Some matters may be referred to the training manager or Human Resources manager for further planning and negotiation of goals and resources.)

3.4 Realistic

You need to ensure that your objectives are achievable, taking into account the various constraints under which you operate – time, resources, ability and current commitments. Break the objectives down into smaller, manageable chunks, if necessary.

3.5 Time-bounded

Include a timescale within which the objective is to be achieved. 'To complete Level 3 Spreadsheets' is the start of an objective but is this within a two-year timescale or a ten-year timescale? 'To complete spreadsheet training within six months (or by a particular date)' is a much better development objective. Make sure your timescale is realistic, too!

4 Learning and development approaches

Your learning objectives will in most cases involve acquiring new skills and knowledge for current and future job challenges. So how will you go about this? It will require research into specific opportunities relevant to your SMART objectives, but some of the sources of CPD you may consider are as follows.

4.1 Technical briefings and updates

If you want to enhance your knowledge on a topic relevant to your work, or to keep your knowledge up to date, you might seek out technical briefings and updates. These may be provided by technical experts within your organisation, or by external bodies. HM Revenue & Customs, for example, may offer update seminars on topics such as VAT, payroll, income/corporate tax, and online reporting. Professional bodies (such as AAT, CIMA and ICAEW) similarly offer technical seminars and local branch events on topics relevant to their field.

You should also look out for technical briefings and updates provided by such bodies in printed form (mailed or emailed to subscribers), or posted on their websites. Your organisation may keep a library of such resources.

4.2 Training courses and seminars

Courses or seminars on technical and wider topics (eg management skills) may be run internally by your organisation. Alternately, external courses can be researched by contacting a local college of further education or by using the internet.

They may be short, stand-alone knowledge- or skills-based courses (eg a course in effective communication, team leadership or using spreadsheets), or they may be part of a longer scheme of study towards an academic, vocational or professional qualification.

The key advantage of training courses is that they generally give you access to experts, in a structured environment which is designed to maximise learning. There is a disadvantage to 'off the job' learning, however, in that it may not be easy to transfer or apply what you have learned in the workplace and of course it tends to be expensive for your organisation.

4.3 The internet

The internet can be used to find details of local course providers and CPD events. It may also be a source of information relevant to your learning needs. For example, you could use a search engine such as Google to find articles on assertiveness or managing conflict in the workplace; websites offering technical and legal updates; or tips and tools for various accounting tasks. There may also be web-based courses (or e-learning) in your areas of interest.

4.4 Publications

Most industries and professions have specialist journals or trade publications, which may include articles relevant to your learning needs. It may be worth subscribing to a publication of this kind, in order to keep up to date with developments in your profession and business sector. Your organisation or department may have a library of relevant journals that you could use, or you may be able to browse the online versions.

Books are another useful learning tool. If you have doubts about your double entry bookkeeping skills, for example, one option is to invest in a textbook and work through it in your own time.

4.5 Other research tools

In addition to information searches in publications and the internet, you might consider research tools such as arranging to talk to (or get instruction from) experts in a topic or skill, or visiting work sites and other places where relevant procedures and practices are demonstrated.

You might also seek out opportunities to try out skills or procedures yourself (where it is not too great a risk to yourself or others to do so!), and then gather feedback on your performance and what you need to do better or differently next time: this is called 'experiential learning' or learning by doing. It is an important tool for on the job learning.

4.6 Colleagues and coaches

One of the most neglected sources of information and learning is work colleagues. They may be able to give you advice on training courses to attend or books or journals to read. You may also be able to learn new skills from colleagues, through instruction or coaching. Don't forget the 'phone a friend' option!

You may find that you can also simply watch more experienced colleagues at work, to learn from their methods, procedures, techniques and behaviour. This observation may take place informally as you work with colleagues, or on a more formal 'shadowing' or coaching basis.

Activity 3: Training approaches

Required

Select the most appropriate learning or training approach for each of the following learning needs.

Learning needs	Suitable approach	
An accounts clerk wishes to work towards becoming AAT qualified.		▼
A worker is transferred onto a new piece of equipment and needs to learn how to operate it.		▼
A new member of staff is about to join the organisation.		▼
An organisation decides that its supervisors would benefit from leadership training.		▼

Picklist:

External training course
Induction training
Internal training course
On the job training

5 Monitoring and reviewing your progress

There is no point in setting an objective if you are not prepared to review your progress and achievements on a regular basis. Regular monitoring and review is important in:

- Allowing you to measure your progress towards your goal, so that you are motivated to 'keep on track'

- Allowing you to identify any mistakes or weaknesses in your current performance, so that you can use them in your learning

- Identifying where you are 'off track' or 'behind schedule' on your development plan, so that you can adjust your effort and activity as required

- Identifying where your goals or plans were unrealistic and need adjustment

- Keeping you accountable to your supervisor, coach or line manager for agreed learning goals and progress

- Enabling your supervisor or line manager to justify the costs of your training and development, in terms of proven results and benefits

- Ensuring that the costs of training and development are not being wasted or used inefficiently

- Ensuring that measurable business benefits are accruing to the organisation from your development

- Enabling you to celebrate improvements and attainments (an important part of staying motivated – and reaping the benefits of development)

5.1 Informally monitoring progress

You can monitor your own progress against your goals on a regular basis. For example, have you kept up to date in your reading on technical changes that affect your job? Have you booked yourself onto the training course that you decided would be a necessary part of your personal development? Are you having to ask for help less frequently? Have you attained the targets you set?

Another review method is to get informal feedback from your supervisor or colleagues. Have they noticed a change in your performance or behaviour? Do they think you have met the targets you set for yourself? How do they think you have improved – and could improve still further?

5.2 Formal evaluation and review

In many cases, there will be more formal methods of evaluation and review. Most organisations plan periodic progress reviews (especially in project work and for new recruits). There will also probably be annual performance appraisal for all employees.

You can also use a **Personal Development Plan** (discussed in a moment) to:

- Set specific criteria for measurement of your progress and attainment

- Gain the co-operation of your supervisor or coach in reviewing your progress at defined intervals or times, and giving you helpful feedback on your progress and performance

- Gain the co-operation of your supervisor in arranging formal testing of your progress or attainment (eg competence assessment, or on the job observation)

Such mechanisms allow you systematically to measure your progress against agreed goals, get feedback from your supervisor (and other relevant parties), review your learning objectives, and identify and agree further learning needs.

6 Your Personal Development Plan

Having come this far, you have all the tools necessary to formulate a more formal and systematic Personal Development Plan or PDP.

A PDP is a clear developmental action plan which, once agreed with the individual's supervisor, acts as a 'learning contract' between them.

You may have your own preferences for formatting and recording action plans: timetables, diaries, checklists and other methods mentioned earlier. Be sure to use any format recommended by your organisation.

In the absence of such guidelines, feel free to use whatever works for you – but we recommend a simple, systematic format such as the following.

Objective	Methods	Timescale	Monitoring/review
Concise statement of your SMART learning objective	Specific learning methods and activities selected	Target completion date for each listed learning method or activity	How, with whom and how often you will check your progress

---

Illustration 3: Personal Development Plan

Back at Southfield Electronics, having identified some immediate learning needs to improve your job performance, you prepare the following Personal Development Plan for the next six months, which you agree with Kellie McDonald (your designated Learning Supervisor).

BPP
LEARNING MEDIA

Objective	Method	Timescale	Monitoring/review
To be able to perform petty cash operations	Coaching: instruction and supervised practice with the cashier	By last week of September	Practice tasks under the cashier's supervision and seek feedback
To be able to perform double entry book-keeping tasks with 100% accuracy, without assistance	Reading: review *Basic Accounting* textbook Training: short external bookkeeping course	By last week of October Completed by last week of October	Practice tasks, checked by Kellie McDonald End of course competency test
To be able to perform receivables ledger reconciliations efficiently, without assistance	Reading: review *Basic Accounting* textbook Coaching: ask Kellie McDonald to instruct and coach me on the process	First week of November By third week of November	Review progress with Kellie during coaching Practice at end October, and seek feedback from Kellie
To achieve the Level 3 Spreadsheets qualification	Training: short computer spreadsheet course	Completed by end of February	End of course competency test Feedback from Ron Howard on application at work

Including your supervisor or line manager in the planning process

Personal Development Planning puts the onus on the individual to define development goals which are relevant to them, and to seek out learning opportunities which suit their needs, preferences and opportunities.

However, it is vitally important to include your supervisor, line manager or designated coach in the process, so that they can:

- Check that your goals are SMART, and of potential benefit to the department and organisation
- Check that the learning activities selected are suitable and cost effective for the organisation
- Suggest learning methods and opportunities that you might not be aware of

- Mobilise learning opportunities and resources (eg by recommending you for a training course, providing access to publications, or appointing a coach or mentor)

- Authorise and arrange the time off and expenditure that will be required for your training (including cover for your absences, where relevant)

- Plan to participate, as required, in your learning (eg by acting as a coach or providing feedback) and in monitoring and review of your progress

Recording your CPD activity

As we noted at the beginning of this chapter, members of professional bodies are required to complete a certain number of hours of CPD, in order to ensure that they maintain their technical competence and up to date knowledge. You must therefore record any CPD activity you undertake, so that you can prove that you have fulfilled the requirements and updated your knowledge and skills appropriately.

Online tools for recording CPD activity are available to AAT members via the AAT website.

Illustration 4: CPD log

Southfield Electronics encourages all accounts staff to maintain a CPD log, which is reviewed alongside each individual's Personal Development Plan. The company uses a simple pro forma log sheet for CPD activity.

CONTINUING PROFESSIONAL DEVELOPMENT RECORD

Name:.. Membership no: ....

Covering the period from: .... to ....

Date(s)	CPD hours	Links to PDP goal	Learning activity	Training provider	Outcomes/ benefits	Follow-up required

> **Assessment focus point**
>
> The assessment may focus on two areas – personal development and professional development (CPD).
>
> For the former, be prepared to carefully read a scenario highlighting a person's needs, and then identify relevant activities.
>
> For the latter, the focus may be on professional requirements for CPD, the benefits to employee and employer, and useful activities.

6.1 Continuing Professional Development: a continuous process!

Just to finish this chapter it should be noted that the setting of personal development objectives, their review, appraisal and updating will be a continuous process throughout your working career – not simply a one-off exercise!

- You need to maintain and update your knowledge and skills to keep pace with technical, legal, technological and other developments affecting your profession and job role. This is called Continuing Professional Development, and it is compulsory for members of professional bodies, as a condition of membership.

- It is important to be able to justify the costs and time devoted to training and development activity. Learning benefits the individual and their employing organisation in a wide variety of ways.

- When considering your own development needs, the best starting point is the current job that you perform. What additional skills or knowledge do you require to carry out your role more effectively and efficiently? What strengths and weaknesses can you identify in the way you fulfil the requirements of your job, as defined by your job description and/or person specification?

- Most employees will have ambitions for career development. Consider your own career goals and what additional skills and knowledge will be required in order for you to achieve them. Remember to be realistic.

- Begin to set your own personal development objectives. Check that they are SMART – specific, measurable, agreed, realistic and time-bounded.

- Sources of CPD activity include technical updates, training courses and seminars, the internet, journals and trade publications, books, colleagues and observation of others.

- Once personal development objectives have been set, progress must be monitored, reviewed and evaluated. This may be a process of self-review, feedback from others or formal appraisal.

- Be prepared to formulate a Personal Development Plan for your own role, based on your own identified career goals, competences, strengths and weaknesses.

Keywords

- **Career goals:** Your aims in terms of the job(s) you aspire to in future

- **Continuing Professional Development:** A process of gaining experience and training relevant to the directions in which you want to develop

- **Development:** Growth in your knowledge and capabilities, and increasing fulfilment of your potential

- **Job description:** A concise statement of the tasks and responsibilities of a particular job

- **Performance appraisal:** The formal process of regular review of each individual employee's performance, progress and development objectives

- **Personal Development Plan:** A learning plan that can be agreed and monitored by your supervisor or learning coach

- **Person specification:** A concise statement of the qualities an organisation wants in the holder of a particular job

- **SMART:** A framework for setting objectives: they should be specific, measurable, agreed, realistic, time-bounded

- **Training:** A planned process of using learning experiences to achieve more effective performance; in particular, work activities or roles

1 **Why is CPD important for members of professional bodies?**

2 **Which of the following are potential benefits of learning and development for an individual employee?**

	✓
Enables improved job performance	☐
It saves time in the short term	☐
Potential for increased rewards and recognition	☐
Greater job security	☐
Decreased job satisfaction	☐
Valuable in the external job market	☐

3 **Excluding the internet, briefly explain any four methods for acquiring new skills and knowledge for your work.**

4 The internet is a good source of technical information, including information on new laws and regulations. However, if the user is not vigilant they could end up obtaining misleading or incorrect technical knowledge.

   Describe why this problem arises when using the internet as a source for this information and outline the precautions you could take to prevent this from happening.

5 **Explain four different ways of monitoring and reviewing your progress against your development goals.**

Understanding ethical and sustainable values

8

Learning outcomes

4.1	Demonstrate an understanding of corporate social responsibility (CSR)
	• Know what CSR is
	• Know organisational actions that support CSR
	• Know good practice in organisations with a strong CSR commitment
4.2	**Identify how finance staff can support ethical business practices**
	• Know how to maintain confidentiality of information
	• Know how to behave professionally in finance: acting with honesty and fairness, ensuring that professional knowledge is up to date
4.3	**Establish the features and benefits of sustainable business practices**
	• Know areas of sustainability: economic, social, environmental
	• Know organisational actions that support sustainability
	• Understand the impact of sustainability activities on the organisation: costs, benefits
	• Understand the impact of sustainability activities outside the organisation: on stakeholders, on the environment, on society

Assessment context

Ethics and sustainability are important parts of the unit syllabus, and are very likely to be examined. For ethics the assessment may focus on the five fundamental principles, as well as scenarios where conflicts of interest arise. For sustainability, tasks may test relevant actions contributing to economic, social and environmental issues to be identified.

Qualification context

This chapter focuses on corporate social responsibility, which includes ethics and sustainability. It is not directly linked to any of the other topics in this unit. It will provide the foundations for the *Ethics for Accountants* unit at Level 3.

Business context

Being aware of corporate social responsibility has become a common issue for most businesses. Employees that are aware of the issues will be better placed to help a business achieve their objectives regarding CSR. In turn this will benefit relationships with stakeholders, including staff and customers, with the potential to increase efficiency and profitability.

Chapter overview

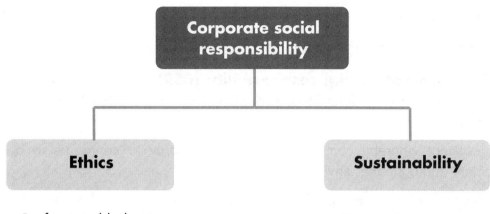

- Professional behaviour
- Objectivity
- Professional competence
- Integrity
- Confidentiality

- Economic aspects
- Social aspects
- Environmental aspects

Introduction

Our final chapter looks at how ethical values fit into the role of the finance professional. We also discuss how individuals, and organisations have a responsibility to act in a sustainable manner.

1 Corporate social responsibility

As a term, **corporate social responsibility (CSR)** has been in use since the 1960s, and has varying definitions, two of which are provided by the European Commission:

- A concept whereby companies decide voluntarily to contribute to a better society and a cleaner environment

- A concept whereby companies integrate social and environmental concerns in their business operations and in their interaction with their stakeholders on a voluntary basis.(European Commission, 2001)

In legal terms a company, for example, is regarded as an entity separate from its owners and, due to recognition of this principle, companies and other organisations are increasingly held accountable for their actions. In the UK, and elsewhere, CSR is largely self-regulated by corporations, in accordance with guidelines, rather than laws.

However, the Companies Act 2006 does give directors a duty to have regard to community and environmental issues, when carrying out their duty to promote the success of a company. Many organisations will now have a CSR policy, which guides their staff in taking responsible actions.

Having a CSR policy can be seen as a positive public relations strategy, leading to business benefits. On the other hand, not acting in a responsible way can have negative business effects as may be seen in the recent Volkswagen vehicle emissions situation, resulting in large repair costs, as well as poor public relations.

While CSR may improve the **ethics** and **sustainability** of a business, it is not enough to guarantee its success, as was illustrated by the collapse of the Enron Corporation, which gained awards for its CSR work, but collapsed due to a large-scale fraud.

2 What are ethics?

Ethics are a set of moral principles that guide behaviour.

Ethical values are assumptions and beliefs about what constitutes 'right' and 'wrong' behaviour.

Individuals have ethical values, often reflecting the beliefs of the families, cultures and educational environments in which they developed their ideas.

Organisations also have ethical values, based on the norms and standards of behaviour that their leaders believe will best help them express their identity and achieve their objectives.

The concept of **business ethics** suggests that businesses are morally responsible for their actions, and should be held accountable for the effects of their actions on people and society.

Some of these ethical values may be explicit: included in the organisation's mission statement, set out in ethical codes and guidelines, or taught in employee training programmes. Other values may be part of the **organisation culture**: 'the way we do things around here', the unwritten rules and customs of behaviour that develop over time as people find ways of working together.

A **code of ethics** often focuses on social issues. It may set out general principles about an organisation's beliefs on matters such as mission, quality, privacy or the environment. The effectiveness of such codes of ethics depends on the extent to which management supports them 'from the top'. The code of ethics often gives rise to a **code of conduct** for employees.

Activity 1: Your ethics

Think of some examples of the kinds of behaviour that you consider 'right' or 'wrong' in your personal and professional life.

2.1 Why behave ethically?

The **AAT Code of Professional Ethics** (the AAT Code) was initiated on 1 September 2011, and revised in 2013. It is based on the **Code of Ethics for Professional Accountants** produced by the International Ethics Standards Board for Accountants (IESBA) of the International Federation of Accountants (IFAC). The AAT is an associate member (not a full member or affiliate) of IFAC.

The AAT Code (2014) notes that: 'the decisions you make in the everyday course of your professional lives can have real ethical implications'.

There are several key reasons why an accounting technician should strive to behave ethically:

- Ethical issues may be a matter of **law and regulation**. You are expected to know and apply the **civil and criminal law** of the country in which you live and work – as a basic minimum requirement for good practice. The AAT Code is based on the laws effective in the UK, with which members are expected to comply as a minimum requirement. (It is sometimes said that 'the law is a floor': the lowest acceptable level of behaviour required to preserve the public interest and individual rights.)

- The **AAT** (like other professional bodies) requires its members to conduct themselves, and provide services to clients, according to certain professional and ethical standards. It does this, in part, to maintain its own **reputation and standing** – but this is also of benefit to its members and to the accounting profession as a whole.

- Professional and ethical behaviour protects the **public interest**. The accountancy profession sees itself as having duties to society as a whole – in addition to its specific obligations to employers and clients.

The AAT Code (2014) advises its members, in a nutshell, as follows:

- Completely avoid even the appearance of **conflict of interest**.

- Be **objective** and act in the **public interest**, because your responsibility is not exclusively to satisfy the needs of an individual client or employer.

- Keep sensitive information **confidential**. Accountants often deal with their employer's or client's most private material.

- Be **straightforward and honest** in professional and business relationships.

- Maintain **professional knowledge, behaviour and skills** at the level required by a client or employer.

- Act within the **spirit and the letter of the law** so as not to bring the profession into disrepute.

2.2 Fundamental ethical principles

You might have your own ideas about what is 'ethical behaviour'. These ideas will be shaped by your personal assumptions and values, and the values of the culture in which you operate (at work and in the country in which you live). However, there are five **fundamental principles** set out in the AAT Code that underpin ethical behaviour in an accounting context:

Fundamental principle	Explanation
Integrity	A member shall be 'straightforward and honest in all professional and business relationships'.
Objectivity	A member shall 'not allow bias, conflict of interest or undue influence of others to override professional or business judgements'.
Professional competence and due care	A member has a continuing duty 'to maintain professional knowledge and skill at the level required to ensure that a client or employer receives competent professional service based on current developments in practice, legislation and techniques. A member shall act diligently and in accordance with applicable and professional standards when providing professional services'

Fundamental principle	Explanation
Confidentiality	A member shall, 'in accordance with the law, respect the confidentiality of information acquired as a result of professional and business relationships and not disclose any such information to third parties without proper and specific authority, unless there is a legal or professional right or duty to disclose. Confidential information acquired as a result of professional and business relationships shall not be used for the personal advantage of the member or third parties'.
Professional behaviour	A member shall 'comply with relevant laws and regulations and avoid any action that brings our profession into disrepute'.

(AAT Code, 2014, para 100.5)

Let's look at each of these in turn:

2.2.1 Integrity

On an everyday level, integrity involves matters such as being **open** about the limitations of your knowledge or competence, being **honest** in your relationships and carrying out your work **accurately, conscientiously and efficiently**.

2.2.2 Objectivity

This is a very important principle for the accounting profession because it protects the interests both of the parties directly affected by an accountant's services and of the general public (who rely on the accuracy of information and the integrity of financial systems).

Objectivity is the principle that all professional and business judgements should be made fairly:

*   On the basis of an **independent** and intellectually honest appraisal of information

*   **Free from** all forms of **prejudice** and **bias**

*   Free from factors which might affect **impartiality**, such as pressure from a superior, financial interest in the outcome, a personal or professional relationship with one of the parties involved, or a conflict of interest (where one client stands to lose and another to gain by a particular disclosure)

Activity 2: Objectivity

A member who is straightforward and honest in all business and professional relationships can be said to be following the fundamental principle of objectivity.

Required: Tick the correct box

	✓
True	
False	

2.2.3 Professional competence and due care

Accountants have an obligation to their employers and clients to know what they are doing – and to do it right!

You should understand that you must not agree to carry out a task or assignment if you do not have the competence to carry it out to a **satisfactory standard** – unless you are sure that you will be able to get the help and advice you need to do so. And if you discover in the course of performing a task or assignment that you lack the knowledge or competence to complete it satisfactorily, you should not continue without taking steps to get the help you need.

In addition, once you have become a member of the profession, you need to maintain and develop your **professional and technical competence**, to keep pace with the demands which may be made on you in your work and developments which may affect your work over time. This may mean:

- Regularly reviewing your working practices against national and international standards, codes, regulations and legislation. Are you complying with the latest requirements?

- Continually upgrading your knowledge and skills in line with developments in accounting practices, requirements and techniques – and making sure that you do not get 'rusty' in the skills you have!

Activity 3: Competence

Identify the appropriate word to use in the following sentence:

'Continuing Professional Development (CPD) is important to accountancy professionals as it helps them [　　　　　▼] competence in their role.'

Picklist:

attain
maintain

BPP
LEARNING MEDIA

Due care is a legal concept that means that, having agreed to do a task or assignment, you have an obligation to carry it out to the best of your ability, in the client's or employer's best interests, within a reasonable timescale and with proper regard for the technical and professional standards expected of you as a professional.

As someone who is knowledgeable about accountancy, you may often deal with others who have little knowledge of accounting matters. This puts you in a position of power, which must never be abused by carrying out your task or assignment in a negligent or 'careless' way.

2.2.4 Confidentiality

Confidentiality is a very important fundamental principle but there are circumstances where the law **allows or requires** that confidentiality to be breached. These circumstances are described in the AAT Code in Section 140.7 and are summarised in the table below.

Circumstance	Examples
'Disclosure is permitted by law and is authorised by the client or employer.'	Providing working papers to a new firm which is taking on the client
'Disclosure is required by law.'	Providing documents or other evidence for legal proceedings Disclosure to HMRC Disclosure of actual/suspected money laundering or terrorist financing to the firm's Money Laundering Reporting Officer (MLRO) or to the National Crime Agency (NCA)
'There is a professional right or duty to disclose which is in the public interest and is not prohibited by law.'	Complying with the quality review of an IFAC member body or other professional body Responding to an inquiry or investigation by the AAT or other regulatory or professional body Disclosure to protect the member's professional interests in legal proceedings Disclosure made to comply with technical standards and ethics requirements

(AAT Code, 2014, para 140.7)

It is vital to appreciate the importance of the fundamental principle of **confidentiality**. You need to respect the confidentiality of information acquired as a result of professional and business relationships. This means that you will not use or disclose confidential information to others, unless:

- You have **specific** and **'proper' authorisation** to do so by the client or employer
- You are legally or professionally **entitled** or **obliged** to do so

(AAT, 2014)

It is also worth being aware that personal information shared with you by clients and colleagues at work should be regarded as confidential, unless you are told otherwise: this is an important basis for trust in any working relationship.

Activity 4: Confidentiality

In which of the following circumstances do you have a legal duty to disclose confidential information concerning a customer of your organisation?

	✓
If they are asked for during legal proceedings	
When your manager tells you to disclose the information	
When writing a report for general circulation within your organisation	

2.2.5 Professional behaviour

The final fundamental principle is professional behaviour.

An example is when advertising their services, members must ensure that they are honest and truthful. They can bring the profession into disrepute by making **exaggerated claims** about services, their qualifications and experience, or if they make **disparaging references or unsubstantiated comparisons** to the work of others.

Applying this principle means **'being professional'**. You'll have your own ideas about what 'being professional' means. Certainly it involves complying with the law and behaving in a way that maintains or enhances the reputation of your profession: bringing it credit – not discredit.

One key aspect of this is **courtesy**. As a professional, you should behave with courtesy and consideration towards anyone you come into contact with in the course of your work and indeed in your personal life.

> **It is impossible for us to overstate the importance of each of these fundamental principles – you MUST be able to recognise each of them.**

Illustration 1: Identifying issues

Now that we've considered the fundamental principles in general, let's consider some typical scenarios in which they might be helpful. In each case, we will identify the ethical issues they present, in line with the basic principles discussed so far. For the purposes of these questions you should assume you are an AAT student.

Incident one

You are asked to produce an aged receivables' listing for your manager as soon as possible. However, you do not have up to date figures because of a problem with the computer system. A colleague suggests that to get the report done in time you use averages for the missing figures.

There is an **integrity** issue here. Using averages instead of actual figures will almost certainly result in an inaccurate listing. You should report the problem to your manager and ask for an extension to your deadline in order to provide an accurate listing.

Incident two

You have received a letter from an estate agent, requesting financial information about one of your company's customers that is applying to rent a property. The information is needed as soon as possible, by fax or email, in order to secure approval for the rent agreement.

There is a **confidentiality** issue here. You need the customer's authority to disclose the information; you may also need to confirm the identity of the person making the request. You should also take steps to protect the confidentiality of the information when you send it: for example, not using fax or email (which can be intercepted), and stating clearly that the information is confidential.

Incident three

While out to lunch, you run into a friend at the sandwich bar. In conversation, she tells you that she expects to inherit from a recently deceased uncle, and asks you how she will be affected by inheritance tax, capital gains tax and other matters.

There are issues of **professional competence and due care** here. You are not qualified to give advice on matters of taxation. Even if you were qualified, any answer you give on the spot would risk being incomplete or inaccurate with potentially serious consequences.

Incident four

A client of the accountancy practice you work in is so pleased with the service you gave him this year that he offers you a free weekend break in a luxury hotel, just as a 'thank you'.

There is an **objectivity** issue here, as the gift is of significant value. Think about how it looks: a third-party observer is entitled to wonder what 'special favours' deserve this extra reward – and/or how such a gift may bias you in the client's favour in future.

3 Conflicts of interest

It is impossible to give guidelines on every possible situation that may arise in the course of your work which conflicts with the fundamental ethical principles. The AAT Code therefore sets out a basic problem-solving procedure, which you can use in any situation, to give yourself the best chance of complying with the principles. This procedure forms the 'conceptual framework' which requires the following:

- Identify where there may be a **threat** to a fundamental principle.

- Evaluate the threat: how significant is it?

- For any significant threat apply **safeguards** that will eliminate the threat or reduce it to an acceptable level (so that compliance with the fundamental principle is not compromised).

- If safeguards cannot be applied, decline or discontinue the specific action or professional service involved or, where necessary, resign from the client (if you are a member in practice) or the employing organisation (if you are a member in business).

Identifying and evaluating threats and the application of safeguards all require the application of an accountant's **professional judgement**. Although professional judgement is a **personal view**, based on an accountant's training and experience, it is expected that all members of the profession would act in a broadly similar way given the same circumstances.

We shall now look at threats and safeguards in more detail.

3.1 Threats

Many of the threats that may create a risk of compromising the fundamental principles will fall into one of the following five categories.

Threat	Explanation	Examples
Self-interest	'Financial or other interests will inappropriately influence the member's judgement or behaviour'	Undue fee dependence on one particular client
Self-review	'A previous judgement needs to be re-evaluated by the member responsible for that judgement'	Tax and accountancy work carried out by the same engagement team
Advocacy	'A member promotes a position or opinion to the point that subsequent objectivity may be compromised'	Acting on behalf of an assurance client which is in litigation or dispute with a third party

Threat	Explanation	Examples
Familiarity	Due to 'a close or personal relationship, a member becomes too sympathetic to the interests of others'	A senior member undertaking an assurance engagement for a number of years for the same client
Intimidation	'A member may be deterred from acting objectively by threats' (actual or perceived)	Threatened withdrawal of services by a dominant client

(AAT Code, 2014, para 200.5 to 200.9)

3.2 Safeguards

The AAT Code (2014) defines safeguards as **'actions or other measures that may eliminate threats or reduce them to an acceptable level'**. The Code identifies two broad categories of safeguards that you might use to reduce or eliminate the threats we have described above.

- Safeguards created by the profession and/or legislation and regulation. These include:

    - Education, training and experience, as requirements for entry into the profession

    - CPD

    - Corporate governance regulations

    - Professional standards

    - Professional or regulatory monitoring and disciplinary procedures

    - External review of financial reports, returns, communications or information produced by members

- **Safeguards in the work environment**, which increase the likelihood of identifying or deterring unethical behaviour, include:

    - Quality controls, and internal audits of quality controls

    - Mechanisms to empower and protect staff who raise ethical concerns ('whistleblowers')

    - Involvement of, or consultation with, independent third parties (eg non-executive directors or regulatory bodies)

    - Rotation of personnel to avoid excessive familiarity and opportunities for collusion in fraud

    - Opportunities to discuss ethical dilemmas (eg with an ethics officer, committee or forum)

Activity 5: Threats

Jake has been put under significant pressure by his manager to change the conclusion of a report he has written which reflects badly on the manager's performance.

Which threat is Jake facing?

	✓
Self-interest	
Advocacy	
Intimidation	

4 Compliance with the law

In the UK, law falls into two categories:

- **Criminal law** – offences relating to persons or property that affect the whole community. Criminal punishment for breach of criminal law (for theft, money laundering, terrorist financing, bribery or fraud, for example) is most likely to result in fines or imprisonment imposed by the State. Criminal cases are **prosecuted** in a criminal court.

- **Civil law** – wrongs relating to conflicts between individuals within the community. There is no involvement of the State. Lawsuits, for breach of contract, negligence and trust, for example, are civil actions and the remedies awarded are designed to place the injured party in the position they would be in were it not for the breach. The concept of punishment does not apply. Civil cases are **heard** in a civil court.

Accountants are affected by a range of laws which they should be aware of. Some of them are not necessarily obvious such as **health and safety legislation**, and **employment protection and equality laws**.

- Members who are employees have duties under health and safety legislation to take precautions against risk of injury and to report potential risks to management. Members who are self-employed have duties to protect the health and safety of their employees.

- All employees have a general duty to behave in ways that contribute to, and maintain, a healthy and safe workplace. Reckless behaviour endangers both yourself and others: creating the risk of accidents, fire, security breach and so on.

- Employment protection and equality laws concern rules on whether an employer can dismiss employees without being liable for claims for wrongful and unfair dismissal. It also includes legislation on treating employees fairly, for example without discriminating against them due to their age, sex, religion or sexual orientation.

Remember, when deciding whether or not behaviour is ethical, compliance with the law is assumed as a starting point: 'the law is a floor'.

5 Business ethics and professional values

In *Setting the Tone: Ethical Business Leadership* by Philippa Foster Back (2005) the author lists some key business values such as truth, transparency, fairness, responsibility and trust.

The importance of business values in a company's culture is that they underpin both policy and behaviour throughout the company, from top to bottom.

Managers usually have a duty to aim for profit. At the same time, modern ethical standards require them to protect the rights of a range of groups inside and outside the organisation who have a legitimate interest or 'stake' in the organisation's activities. These groups are often known as **stakeholders**.

Business ethics are also relevant to **competitive behaviour**: there is a distinction between competing aggressively and competing unethically (for example, by stealing competitors' designs; using buyer power to prevent suppliers from dealing with competitors; or spreading false negative information about competitors).

A consequence of the need for a business to act ethically may be for it to **change its culture** so all employees, managers and directors know that ethical behaviour is expected of them and that the management will take action against unethical behaviour. For example, management might 'turn a blind eye' to employees submitting inflated expense claims, but this is not something an ethical organisation would allow. Therefore the attitude of employees and managers must be changed so that only accurate expense claims are made.

To achieve this, a **code of conduct** must be developed and 'sold' to the organisation. The **Institute of Business Ethics** (IBE) was set up in 1986 to encourage high standards of business behaviour based on ethical values.

The IBE's website contains a lot of information on the purpose of ethics policies and programmes and also how to develop a code of ethics and make it work within an organisation.

The IBE also sets out the simple ethical tests for a business decision. Some companies provide their employees with ethical tests to help them make decisions, ie a series of questions to ask themselves. The IBE's simple ethical tests for a business decision are:

- **Transparency** ('Do I mind others knowing what I have decided?')
- **Effect** ('Who does my decision affect or hurt?')
- **Fairness** ('Would my decision be considered fair by those affected?')

6 Sustainability

We saw earlier that accountants are expected to act in the public interest and, in the modern business world, the concept of **sustainability** is increasingly important in this regard.

There are three aspects to sustainability.

Economic sustainability ensures fair distribution and efficient allocation of global resources. Developed countries consume more per capita than developing countries. Economic growth must be balanced with the needs of the developing world.

Social sustainability involves the responsibility to work towards eradication of human inequality, poverty and social injustice. This responsibility falls particularly heavily on Western firms that employ people in developing countries.

Environmental sustainability describes the need for organisations to consider how their activities impact the environment and to take steps to minimise that impact and to conserve energy.

Sustainable development is a core part of an organisation's **CSR**. It can be seen in policies aimed at reducing waste, using less energy and recycling. Companies are increasingly engaging in practices such as encouraging flexible working, cycle to work schemes, reducing business travel through the use of technology and sourcing materials from green suppliers. Sustainability is also fostered through research and development, supply chain improvements and innovation.

Another definition of sustainability can be found in the **UN's Brundtland Report** (1987). According to this, organisations must aim to 'meet the needs of the present without compromising the ability of future generations to meet their own needs'.

We shall consider this definition further in the next section.

7 Duties and responsibilities of finance professionals in relation to sustainability

The definition of sustainability from the **UN's Brundtland Report** makes it clear that business organisations have a duty to **protect society** and **future generations**. As part of the business world, finance professionals have a duty to consider the economic, social and environmental aspects of their work in order to support sustainability.

7.1 Duties of finance professionals

The diagram below shows how economic, social and environmental issues are linked.

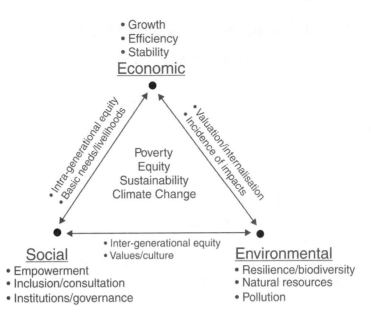

Economic aspects that finance professionals may consider include supporting their organisation or clients to be profitable, supporting local businesses when deciding on suppliers and paying them on time and looking for ways to improve the efficiency of the organisation's finance operations.

Social aspects may include supporting policies on corporate governance and consulting the local community when making decisions on investing in or relocating operations.

Environmental aspects are usually focused on using less energy and creating less pollution. A finance professional should therefore support company policies on the long-term management of resources and facilitating the running of their organisation in a sustainable manner. These may include, for example, not printing emails unless necessary, turning lights off at the end of the day and recycling materials used in their office.

7.2 Responsibilities of finance professionals

There are six main responsibilities of finance professionals in regards to upholding the principles of sustainability.

Creating and promoting a sustainable culture

Finance professionals should help senior management create and promote a sustainable culture within their organisation. Primarily it means supporting sustainable policies as they are introduced, but it also means discouraging wasteful or environmentally unfriendly behaviour if they are aware of it.

Championing the aims of sustainability

The aims of sustainability, as identified by the UN's Brundtland Report, should be promoted and followed. However, the finance professional should remain objective at all times. This means that the aims should not be followed blindly, but instead be followed within the context of the organisation's culture and its own policies on sustainability.

Evaluating and quantifying reputational and other ethical risks

Finance professionals have well-developed analysis and evaluational skills. This means they are among the best placed within an organisation to deal with reputational and other ethical risks, including risks to the environment.

Taking social, environmental and ethical factors into account when making decisions

Social, environmental and ethical factors are together known as the 'triple bottom line'. Many organisations demonstrate their commitment to CSR by including, in their financial reports, organisational performance information based on these factors. Financial professionals have a responsibility to take these factors into account when making decisions so that, when organisational position and performance is measured, the business can clearly demonstrate its commitment to CSR.

Promoting sustainable practices

As well as promoting policies in relation to ethical and illegal practices, finance professionals should support sustainability practices developed by the organisation. Such practices may be in relation to, for example, products and services, customers, employees, the workplace, supply chain and business functions and processes.

Raising awareness of social responsibility

As mentioned earlier, finance professionals should consider the sustainability impacts of their decisions and actions. By doing so, they will help raise awareness of sustainability within the organisation as colleagues, who may be in different departments, see them taking a lead in this area.

Activity 6: Sustainability

Think of some examples of sustainability issues in the place that you work or study.

8 Impact and effects of sustainability

A business may adopt policies and procedures which support sustainability from an environmental and an organisational perspective.

8.1 Environmental perspectives

Environmental areas of focus include the actions an organisation or those within the accounting function can take in respect of:

- Environmental care
- Recycling
- Energy and resource consumption
- Travel efficiencies

8.2 Organisational perspectives

Organisational areas of focus include the actions an organisation takes in respect of:

- Its shareholders
- The acquisition and retention of customers
- The acquisition and retention of suppliers
- Delivery of high-quality goods and services
- Development of employees

8.3 Impacts and effects

In each case, it should be remembered that there may be costs as well as benefits in pursuing a sustainable solution. A business will need to weigh up any additional costs and compare them with the benefits received.

Illustration 2: Costs and benefits

Scenario 1

In seeking to care for the environment, a business may decide to abandon the harsh chemicals used in cleaning the business premises and to use environmentally friendly products instead. However, these new products prove to cost more than the original chemicals. This needs to be compared with the positive publicity generated by caring for the environment and the sales generated by new customers attracted by an environmentally friendly business.

Scenario 2

A business may decide to start using recyclable packaging. Its current supplier cannot supply this and so the business has to find a new supplier. This process will take time and may mean that the business does not receive such good discounts as its current supplier gives it. These costs must be taken into account when considering the benefits of the project.

Scenario 3

A business decides that it will save paper by using electronic methods of communicating with its shareholders. It needs to remember that some shareholders may not have access to computers and could be alienated by this move. Shareholders will need to be given the option to continue to receive paper communications in future. So the costs of polling shareholders and the likely numbers who will opt for paperless communication need to be taken into account.

Activity 7: Identifying issues and aspects

Identify which sustainability initiatives have an environmental aspect:

(a)   Ensuring well-fitted windows and doors to prevent heat loss

(b)   Selecting suppliers who operate fair employment practices

(c)   Encouraging a staff charity committee to help raise funds for local community projects

(d)   Programming movement sensors to turn off unnecessary lighting

(e)   Having monthly team meetings by video conference, rather than requiring staff to travel to one location

---

Assessment focus point

The assessment tasks for this topic will cover a range of situations involving CSR, including ethics and sustainability.

You should know the names of the fundamental ethical principles, the meaning behind each of them and how they can be applied in practice. It will be useful to test yourself with various scenarios to identify the relevant principles.

Do look out for ideas or qualities that are **not** relevant ethical principles, for example:

- Subjectivity, which is the opposite of objectivity

- Accuracy, which while important for accountants is not a 'fundamental principle'

You should be familiar with the three aspects of sustainability. A task could present you with a list of business practices. Most will probably be good business, but consider that only some may be sustainability initiatives. Alternatively you may be given a list of **sustainability** initiatives, and asked to identify which is of environmental, economic or social benefit. If an initiative appears to be a mix, then consider its dominant effect.

Chapter summary

- **Ethical values** are assumptions and beliefs about what constitutes 'right' and 'wrong' behaviour. Individuals, families, national cultures and organisation cultures all develop ethical values and norms.

- **Ethical behaviour** is necessary to comply with law and regulation; to protect the public interest; to protect the reputation and standing of a professional body and its members; and to enable people to live and work together in society.

- The **AAT Code of Professional Ethics** (2014) notes that: 'the decisions you make in the everyday course of your professional lives can have real ethical implications'.

- **The five fundamental principles** described in the AAT Code are:
  - Integrity
  - Objectivity
  - Professional competence and due care
  - Confidentiality
  - Professional behaviour

- The AAT's Code sets out a **basic problem-solving procedure** for unethical action (the 'conceptual framework'):
  - Identify the threat to the fundamental principles that the action represents
  - Evaluate the threat
  - Apply safeguards to eliminate or reduce the threat
  - If safeguards cannot be applied, decline or discontinue the action

- The IBE sets out simple ethical tests for a business decision:
  - Transparency
  - Effect
  - Fairness

- The concept of **business ethics** suggests that businesses and other corporate entities are morally responsible for their actions.

- Key issues in being an **ethical employee and colleague** include not undertaking tasks that are beyond your personal experience and expertise; not undermining your professional colleagues; honesty; and ethical relationships.

- Finance professionals have a duty to protect the public interest and promote **sustainability**. They should consider the **economic**, **social** and **environmental aspects** of their work.

- As part of their role, finance professionals have a number of **responsibilities** in relation to upholding the principles of **sustainability**.

- Each sustainability project will have **costs** as well as **benefits**.

- **Corporate social responsibility (CSR):** A concept whereby companies integrate social and environmental concerns in their business operations and in their interaction with their stakeholders on a voluntary basis

- **Ethics:** A set of moral principles that guide behaviour

- **Sustainability:** Meeting the needs of the present without compromising the ability of future generations to meet their own needs

Test your learning

Respond to the following by selecting the appropriate option.

1 **Only individuals can have 'ethical values'.**

	✓
True	
False	

2 **The AAT needs to protect its reputation and standing by maintaining standards of conduct and service among its members in order to be able to:**

	✓
Enhance the reputation and standing of its members	
Limit the number of members that it has	
Make sure that its members are able to earn large salaries	

3 A client asks you a technical question about accounting standards which you are not sure you are able to answer correctly. 'You are supposed to be an accountant, aren't you?' says the client. 'I need an answer now.' **What should you do first?**

	✓
Say that you will get back to him when you have looked up the answer.	
Give him the contact details of a friend in your firm who knows all about accounting standards.	
Clarify the limits of your expertise with the client.	

4 **Why are professional standards important?**

	✓
It is in the public interest that employees who fail to comply with standards are prosecuted.	
It is in the public interest that services are carried out to professional standards.	

5 **Which one of the following statements best describes sustainability?**

	✓
Policies aimed at improving efficiency including reducing waste, using less energy and recycling	
A long-term programme involving a series of sustainable development practices aimed at improving organisational efficiency, stakeholder support and market edge	
A core part of an organisation's corporate social responsibility comprising efficiency, stakeholder support and market edge	

Activity answers

CHAPTER 1 The role of the financial function

Activity 1: Payroll information

The correct answer is:

Information	Required by payroll from other departments	Provided by payroll to other parties
Total wage/salary and overtime costs		✓
Employees' National Insurance details	✓	
Date of commencement of employment	✓	
Information for individual employees about pay and deductions		✓
Statutory returns to external agencies		✓
Standard and overtime hours worked	✓	
Wage/salary and overtime rates	✓	

Activity 2: Email

The correct answer is:

EMAIL

To: hskommett@southfield.co.uk
From: yourname@southfield.co.uk
Date: | 13/06/X2 |

Subject: Cash flow and credit control issues

I'm sure you know how important it is to maintain | positive | cash flow, so that the organisation has sufficient day to day funds to maintain its operations and pay its | payables |. Recently, however, Southfield has been paying out money to suppliers | faster | than it has been collecting money from customers. The Sales department obviously has a key role in this, through its credit control policies. The Chief Accountant is keen to review this issue with you and the | Purchasing Manager |.

Kind regards

YN

CHAPTER 2 The organisational framework

Activity 1: Organisation charts

(a) You report directly to three people: Kellie McDonald, Ron Howard and Jane Chu.

(b) NI contributions are a payroll matter, so the natural person to consult would be Jane Chu, the Payroll Manager.

(c) The two Assistant Financial Accountants and the Payroll Manager are on the same level of authority.

(d) This might cause you difficulties because, if they make excessive or conflicting work demands on you, it will be difficult to know whose work to prioritise: they all have an equal 'right' to exercise authority over you.

(e) You would need to look further up the chain of command, which leads directly to the Financial Accountant (Jenny Faulkner).

(f) The formal line of communication would be to contact them via the Production Manager.

(g) The finance function only has 'staff' (that is, expert, advisory or policy-making) authority over Logistics in areas to do with finance (such as credit control).

Activity 2: Evacuation procedure

(a) The correct answer is:

Action	Correct/Incorrect
Leave the building by the designated route as quickly (but calmly) as possible, not lingering to gather personal belongings	Correct
Use lifts in the event of a fire emergency	Incorrect
Go immediately to the designated Assembly Point and ensure that any visitors are directed and assisted	Correct
Pay particular attention to people with special needs (eg those in wheelchairs or with impaired sight or hearing)	Correct
Stay quiet when your name is called by the Safety Officer who will 'call a roll' of everyone signed in as being in the building	Incorrect
Do not return to the building until instructed to do so by a senior official or the Safety Officer	Correct

(b) It is very important to take part in drills, and to comply with the procedure when doing so. Repeated practice will make employees better at evacuation – contributing to everyone's safety. There is no way of knowing if an alarm is for a drill or 'for real': by failing to take part and follow the procedure, an employee is endangering their life and the lives of others. Employees should therefore all be responsible for co-operating with the policy.

Activity 3: Providing information

The correct answer is:

	Yes – provide information	No – personal information	No – confidential information
A customer asks for the address and telephone number of another customer	☐	☐	☑
A colleague asks you for the home address of two other employees	☐	☑	☐
The company's security guard asks for the names of the visitors expected by your department that week	☑	☐	☐

Activity 4: Authorisation

You will need to know:

(a) What documents are required (eg appropriate form, attached receipts)

(b) What value of transactions require authorisation, and at what levels

(c) Who the authorising managers or designated signatories are

(d) Deadlines for receipt and authorisation

(e) How transactions should be processed

(f) What you should do if the information is incomplete, incorrectly authorised or otherwise contrary to the policy

CHAPTER 3 Personal skills

Activity 1: Communication mediums

The correct answer is:

Situation	Medium
New stationery is urgently required from the office goods supplier.	Telephone
The Managing Director wants to give a message to all staff.	Notice board/intranet
A member of staff has been absent five times in the past month, and her manager intends to take action.	Face to face conversation
You need information quickly from another department.	Telephone
You have to explain a complicated procedure to a group of people.	Meeting

Activity 2: Word processing

The correct answer is:

Documents can be saved and edited easily. ☑

They provide the personal touch. ☐

The writer can make corrections and changes which are 'invisible' to the reader. ☑

Documents can be tailored to individual circumstances but this takes time – often quicker to write from scratch. ☐

Standard or 'template' documents can be created. ☑

Activity 3: Job description

The correct categories are:

Aggressive	N
Assertive	D
Good communicator	E
Good listener	E
Introvert	N
Respectful	D
Responsible	D
Trustworthy	D

Activity 4: Business style

The correct categories are:

Do...	Don't...
Write in full sentences	Use 'text message' style abbreviations
Use direct, commonly used, and factual language **Note.** Direct–so not ambiguous; Commonly used–so not clichéd; Factual–so less emotional	Use abbreviated forms such as 'There's', 'I'm', 'We've': use the full forms ('There is', 'I am', 'We have') instead
Remove digressions, rambles and unnecessary words and phrases: keep to the point	Use colloquial or slang expressions **Note.** Instead of 'This sucks': use something like 'This is frustrating' or 'This is unsatisfactory'...)
Refer to people by their title and surname, in more formal relationships – or where their expectations about formality are unknown	Be overly 'familiar' or friendly in tone, or personal in content, unless the other person has expressly invited this

Activity 5: Calculations

(a) The correct answer is: 20%

If a training programme costs £2,300 out of a total of £11,500:

$$\frac{2,300}{11,500} \times 100 = \frac{230,000}{1,150,000} = \frac{1}{5} = 20\%$$

(b) The correct answer is: 72 degrees

In a pie chart, this would be 20% of a 360° circle:

$$\frac{20}{100} \times 360 = \text{a } 72° \text{ slice of the circle.}$$

(c) The correct answer is:

Amount of discount £345

Net amount payable £1,955

$$15\% \text{ discount on } £2,300 = \frac{15}{100} \times £2,300 = £345$$

The total net amount payable is £2,300 – £345 = £1,955.

Activity 6: Invoice

The correct answer is: £2,499.00

	£
List price	2,450.00
Less discount £2,450.00 × 15/100	(367.50)
	2,082.50
Plus VAT (£2,082.50 × 20/100)	416.50
	£2,499.00

Activity 7: Averages

(a) The correct answer is:

Provider 1   £400
Provider 2   £376

First, you need to calculate the cost of the Effective Communication courses, so that they fit the rest of the data.

£200 × 3 days = £600   £210 × 2½ days = £525

Using the mean:

Provider 1 = (250 + 590 + 260 + 300 + 600) ÷ 5 courses = 2,000 ÷ 5 = £400.

Provider 2 = (340 + 375 + 290 + 350 + 525) ÷ 5 courses = 1,880 ÷ 5 = £376.

(b) The correct answer is:

    Provider 1   £300
    Provider 2   £350

    Using the median:

    Provider 1 =   250   260   300   590   600   The median is 300.

    Provider 2 =   290   340   350   375   525   The median is 350.

(c) Provider 2 offers the lower average cost based on the mean; however, the median value is lower for Provider 1. This discrepancy occurs because, although some of Provider 1's courses are significantly cheaper than any of Provider 2's (providing a lower middle value for Provider 1), the very high cost of the 'payroll' and 'effective communication' courses result in Provider 1's mean value for all courses being 'skewed', and therefore a higher mean cost than for Provider 2. Someone looking to purchase all 5 courses would get better value from Provider 2. However, for 1 to 4 courses only it is possible that Provider 1 may be cheaper, depending on the courses chosen.

Activity 8: Percentages

The correct answer is:

Anne	15.358%
Jaitinder	24.232%
Benjamin	29.352%
Chloe	10.922%
Vimal	20.137%

Workings

	Travel expense	
	£	**%**
Anne	45/293	15.358
Jaitinder	71/293	24.232
Benjamin	86/293	29.352
Chloe	32/293	10.922
Vimal	59/293	20.137

Activity 1: Graphs and charts

(a) The correct answer is:

Product	Jan £000	Feb £000	Mar £000	Apr £000	May £000	Jun £000	Total £000
A	800	725	725	400	415	405	3,470
B	210	210	180	150	175	160	1,085
C	25	50	60	95	125	140	495
Total	1,035	985	965	645	715	705	5,050

(b) We'd recommend a line graph.

Monthly sales for the first six months of 20X0

(c) We'd recommend a pie chart.

Product A:

3,470/5,050 × 100 = 68.71% = approximately 7/10 of the circle

Product B:

1,085/5,050 × 100 = 21.49% = approximately 1/5 of the circle

Product C:

495/5,050 × 100 = 9.8% = approximately 1/10 of the circle

Proportion of six months' sales

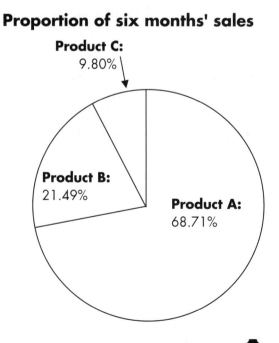

Product C: 9.80%

Product B: 21.49%

Product A: 68.71%

Activity 2: Letter

The correct answers are:

(a)	Dear Sirs	Yours faithfully,
(b)	Dear Ms Brown	Yours sincerely,
(c)	Dear Mark	Kind regards,
(d)	Dear Sir Joshua	Yours sincerely,

Note that (d) is a special case when it is appropriate to use the person's first name in a formal address. It applies to people with the titles Sir X or Lady Y.

Activity 3: Opening lines

(a) 'Following our telephone conversation of [date], I enclose the brochure you requested, which details our services.'

(b) 'I have been asked by my colleague, George Brown, to contact you in regard to your enquiry about career opportunities in the Accounts department of our firm.'

(c) 'I look forward to meeting you to discuss the matter in more detail.'

(d) 'If you require any further information, please do not hesitate to telephone me on the number given above.'

Activity 4: Memo and letter

(a)

SOUTHFIELD ELECTRONICS LTD
MEMORANDUM

To: Jenny Faulkner, Financial Accountant
From: Your Name, Accounts Clerk
Date: 11 September 20X0
Subject: Project re abuse of telephone procedures

I would be very pleased to take on the project of investigating ways to minimise further telephone cost increases. Thank you for the opportunity. I will have to check with Kellie, Ron and Jane, to ensure that there is sufficient flexibility in my workload, but I cannot see that this will be a problem.

My initial thoughts are that we should seek:

(a)   To disconnect handsets that we do not need

(b)   To include telephone usage in the forthcoming briefing on compliance with policy

(c)   To gain some control over staff phone usage, by using a central switchboard or call logging. With your permission, I will start by getting some information about the possibilities from an office equipment provider.

I will keep you informed as the investigation progresses.

YN

(b)

SOUTHFIELD ELECTRONICS LTD

Tomorrow's technology for today's homes

Micro House
Newtown Technology Park
Innovation Way
Middx NT3 OPN

The Sales Manager
TeleComs Ltd
6 Park Way
Brighton
Sussex BN3 4PW

11 September 20X0

Dear Sirs,

Electronic switchboards and call logging devices

I am writing to request information about your models of electronic switchboards and call logging devices, their capabilities and costs.

Southfield Electronics operates a fairly large office, and we are looking to control telephone costs. One of the approaches we will be considering is the monitoring and controlling of outgoing calls. You will no doubt be able to recommend suitable systems for our needs.

In the first instance, please send your information brochure to the office address supplied above. Alternatively, you can send material via email to: yname@southfield.co.uk.

Thank you for your attention. I look forward to hearing from you soon.

Yours faithfully,

Your Name

Your Name

Accounts Clerk

Activity 5: Email

EMAIL

Date: [inserted automatically]
To: yourname@southfield.co.uk
From: alaval@southfield.co.uk
Subject: RE: Customer analysis
Attach: customeranalysis.xls

Your name,

I attach an example of a completed customer analysis, as you requested. You will see that it is an Excel file, as I have formatted the analysis as a spreadsheet.

If you need any other help, let me know.

Amy

CHAPTER 5 Working independently

Activity 1: Routine or unexpected

The correct answer is:

Routine tasks	Unexpected tasks
Performing the weekly bank reconciliation	Preparing a special report for your manager
Preparing sales invoices daily	Showing a visitor around
Listing cheques received in the post each morning	Dealing with petty cash as the petty cashier is off sick

Activity 2: Urgent or important

The correct answer is:

Task	Important/Urgent
Preparing a credit note listing for your manager due by the end of the month	Important
Producing a staff analysis for the Personnel Director for a meeting this afternoon	Urgent
Producing product costings for the Production Manager for a meeting first thing tomorrow morning	Urgent
Checking purchase invoices to goods received notes	Important

Activity 3: Prioritising

The correct answer is: Continue printing the sales invoices.

Both tasks are urgent but the sales invoices are more urgent, as they must be sent out today. The report is not needed until 12:00 noon on Monday so, provided that you make sure you can start the print run by 9:00am on Monday, and agree this with your supervisor, this is the best plan of action.

Activity 4: Scheduling tasks

Thursday tasks	Order of task completion
Generate statement and send to major customer	First task
Respond to customer queries from the day before	Second task
Enter sales invoices/credit notes	Third task
Enter purchase invoices/credit notes	Fourth task
Enter cash receipts and payments	Fifth task
Generate eight customer balances for MD meeting	Sixth task
HR meeting	Seventh task
Print daily cheque run	Eighth task

Notes and workings

The statement is for a key customer who needs it as soon as possible, therefore this task should have been carried out first.

The assistant did not know about the request by the Managing Director (MD) for customer balances and activities until 2:00pm. Although the data was not needed until the following morning, the assistant would not have any time the next day as the meeting is at 9:00am. In addition, the assistant would only have had 30 minutes of her day left after the compulsory meeting, so would need to complete this task before the meeting in order to get it to the MD in advance of the meeting (since it could take up to an hour and a half).

The remaining tasks are fitted in around the urgent tasks and carried out in order of priority. The only one there will not be time for is the filing of invoices and credit notes.

Assuming everything took the maximum estimated time, the order of tasks above would produce a day of tasks as follows.

Task/break	Duration (hrs)	Task order	Time period
Generate statement and send to major customer	0.5	First task	9:00am to 9:30am
Respond to customer queries from the day before	1	Second task	9:30am to 10:30am
Enter sales invoices/credit notes	0.75	Third task	10:30am to 11:15am
Enter purchase invoices/credit notes	0.75	Fourth task	11:15am to 12:00 noon
Enter cash receipts and payments	1	Fifth task	12:00 noon to 1:00pm
Lunch	1		1:00pm to 2:00pm
Generate eight customer balances for MD meeting	1.5	Sixth task	2:00pm to 3:30pm
HR meeting	1	Seventh task	3:30pm to 4:30pm
Print daily cheque run	0.5	Eighth task	4:30pm to 5:00pm

Activity 5: Planning chart

The correct answer is:

Table	Ahead of schedule
Shelves	Behind schedule
Kitchen units	Not due to start
Bed	Completed on schedule

The furniture maker is ahead of schedule in producing the table, having already completed it, even though it was not scheduled for completion until the end of today (Thursday). They are on schedule with the bed, having completed it as planned by the end of Wednesday. However, they are now behind schedule on the shelves, since progress is 'behind' where it should be at the 'time now' line. It may be possible to catch up, since the table maker has spare time to help out the shelf maker. The kitchen units aren't due to be started until tomorrow.

Activity 6: Timetable

TIMETABLE					
	Mon 8	**Tue 9**	**Wed 10**	**Thu 11**	**Fri 12**
[8:00–9:00]	EF2	CD1	AB1	AB2	Train
9:00–10:00	EF2	EF1	AB1	AB3	Train
10:00–11:00	EF2	EF1	AB1	AB3	Train
11:00–12:00	EF2	EF1	AB1	AB3	Train
12:00–13:00					
13:00–14:00	CD1	EF1	AB1	AB3	Train
14:00–15:00	CD1	EF1	AB2	AB3	Train
15:00–16:00	CD1	EF1	AB2	AB3	AB4
16:00–17:00	CD1	AB1	AB2	AB3	AB4
[17:00–18:00]	CD1	AB1	AB2	AB3	AB4

Tasks carried over to week beginning 15 October:

- AB4 (9 hours remaining): Monday 15
- AB5 (2 hours): fit in some time during this week or following

Problem tasks:

- AB2: asked for by end of the day Wednesday, but if I work early overtime, I should be able to complete the task by 9:00am Thursday: check with AB that this is acceptable.

- AB4: asked for by end of the day Monday 15, with nine hours remaining. May not be possible to allocate all nine hours of Monday 15 to this task: need to discuss with AB.

If AB's deadlines are not moveable, I would have to discuss the other tasks with CD and EF to see if there is any flexibility to fit in AB's tasks earlier.

CHAPTER 6 Working as part of a team

Activity 1: Not meeting deadlines

- The work may have to be transferred to other team members, meaning that their plans and schedules will have to be adjusted, and they will end up bearing a heavier share of the total workload.

- One person's failure to meet a deadline may, if there is little 'slack time' in a schedule, result in others failing to meet their deadlines. This causes them frustration and disruption – and may affect the team's ability to complete the whole task on time.

- Failure to 'pull one's weight' or meet agreed deadlines can have an impact on working relationships within the team. Resentment, frustration, blame and conflict may arise.

Activity 2: Assistance and support

The correct answer is: Offer to help input the figures on Thursday

You should not offer to help with analysis on Wednesday, since you do not have spare time on that day. However, you are likely to have some spare time on Thursday, so you should offer to help your colleague to input the figures to the computer then. The entire project depends upon the figures being ready, and you should offer assistance to ensure that the project team meets this deadline. You might check with your departmental supervisor first, however, to ensure that she agrees this is the best use of your time.

Activity 3: Being assertive

You have handled this situation effectively, because you have managed to respect your prior agreements and project deadlines – while still being courteous and co-operative in offering options to Ron Howard.

The key points of the argument are:

- You have made prior commitments, which you wish to respect.

- Breaking your prior commitments, by missing your deadline, will impact on the work of a project team.

- Your prior commitment is to a manager at the same level of authority as Ron, and with the backing of a higher manager (Jenny Faulkner).

- It is not reasonable for Ron to ask you to work long overtime hours so that he can have personal time off: you have a right to say no.

- Ron is still your superior, so you should be calm, respectful and co-operative in your dealings with him.

- You have limited authority to propose alternative options: Ron should settle the matter with Kellie McDonald, since the real problem is between their conflicting demands.

Activity 4: Assertive behaviour

The correct answer is: Standing up for your own rights, needs and opinions.

Activity 5: Conflict resolution

The correct answer is: Find out why each wants the window desk and look for solutions to meet their needs.

If one team member gets the window desk and the other doesn't it will result in resentment and demotivation of the 'losing' member, so this is a win–lose situation.

If the team members get the window desk on alternate days or weeks, this will result in half-satisfied needs, so both lose out (lose–lose).

The only possibility to create a win–win situation is to establish what each wants the window desk for and to look for solutions to satisfy both employees' needs. For example, one may want the view, the other better lighting conditions. This offers options to be explored such as improved lighting being provided for one of the employees.

CHAPTER 7 Developing skills and knowledge

Activity 1: CPD benefits

EMAIL

From:	y.name@reeves.co.uk
To:	a.bolt@reeves.co.uk
Cc:	g.hoff@reeves.co.uk
Date:	*[Today's date]*
Re:	RE: Action Plan

Thank you for your email about the cost of implementing Action Plans and training requests for the Accounts department. Mrs Hoff has asked me to reply on her behalf.

I am sure you are aware that all professional bodies require their members to keep their technical knowledge up to date, as a condition of membership. All members of the Accounts department are therefore bound to complete a certain number of hours of Continuing Professional Development activity, or they will not be able to continue as members of their professional body. This, in turn, would impact on their ability to perform their jobs.

Reeves Ltd will also benefit in many ways from Accounts department CPD activity, in terms of: more competent job performance; less supervision required; increased productivity; reduced risk and cost of errors and non-compliance with regulations/laws; improved staff motivation and morale; and an enhanced ability to recruit and retain professionally qualified staff.

I hope this explains the ambitious Action Plans submitted by the department – and also goes some way to justify the cost and time requirements.

I would be happy to give you more information about CPD requirements, if this would be helpful.

YN.

Activity 2: Job role documents

The correct answer is:

The | person specification | for your role sets out what sort of personal qualities the organisation is looking for in your role.

The | job description | sets out what a person in your job should be able to do.

Activity 3 Training approaches

The correct answer is:

Learning needs	Suitable approach
An accounts clerk wishes to work towards becoming AAT qualified.	External training course
A worker is transferred onto a new piece of equipment and needs to learn how to operate it.	On the job training
A new member of staff is about to join the organisation.	Induction training
An organisation decides that its supervisors would benefit from leadership training.	Internal training course/External training course*

*The ability to train supervisors internally will depend on the availability of suitably experienced management to provide the necessary training. If this is unavailable the organisation may seek to use an external training company.

CHAPTER 8 Understanding ethical and sustainable values

Activity 1: Your ethics

This is personal to you, so that you begin to think about your own assumptions and beliefs about what kinds of behaviour are 'OK' and 'not OK'. Some of these may be in line with the ethical values of the AAT and the accounting profession (such as being honest, telling the truth, being fair and working hard) and some may not be (such as using your work position for the benefit of family members, or offering gifts as a smoother of business relationships and negotiations). In a way, these instances – where your values differ from the professional standards – are more useful information: you know where your 'blind spots' are, and where you may have to modify your assumptions and habits.

Activity 2: Objectivity

The correct answer is:

	✓
True	
False	✓

Straightforwardness and honesty are related to the fundamental principle of integrity.

Activity 3: Competence

Continuing Professional Development (CPD) is important to accountancy professionals as it helps them | maintain | competence in their role.

Accountancy professionals attain competence by passing professional exams and gaining relevant experience. It is the maintenance of professional competence that requires continuing awareness and understanding of relevant technical, professional and business developments and is achieved through CPD.

Activity 4: Confidentiality

The correct answer is:

	✓
If they are asked for during legal proceedings	✓
When your manager tells you to disclose the information	
When writing a report for general circulation within your organisation	

In this case you have a legal duty to disclose the information.

Activity 5: Threats

The correct answer is:

	✓
Self-interest	
Advocacy	
Intimidation	✓

'Significant pressure' indicates intimidation threat.

Activity 6: Sustainability

Your answer will depend on the nature of your job and the type of organisation that you work for. Good answers would include issues relating to economic factors, social factors and the environment.

Activity 7: Identifying issues and aspects

(a)   Environmental – as it reduces fuel consumption (also economic as it saves fuel cost)

(d)   Environmental – as in (a), it also has an economic aspect

(e)   Environmental – less travel is needed, leading to less pollution (also economic aspect as less travel may mean less cost)

Note:

(b)   Social – as it supports people

(c)   Social – as it benefits the local community

Test your learning: answers

Chapter 1

1   The correct answer is:

Human resources   ☑

Manufacturing   ☐

Stores control   ☐

Accounting and finance   ☑

Information technology   ☑

2   The correct answer is:

		Production of financial statements
Financial accounting		Prepares information for internal use
		Processing and recording transactions
Management accounting		Prepares information for external use
		Provides information for managers to make decisions

3   The correct answer is:

The calculation of gross pay   ☑

Purchasing supplies   ☐

The calculation of tax, National Insurance and other deductions   ☑

Preparing payslips   ☑

Bank reconciliations   ☐

Paying cash into the bank   ☐

Making up wages, or preparing data for direct credit (BACS)   ☑

Writing cheques   ☐

Distributing payslips to employees   ☑

4   The correct answer is:

Providing a service at the least possible cost ☐

Minimum wastage ☑

Paying the minimum wage to employees ☐

Achieving objectives with minimum use of resources ☑

5   The correct answer is:

Health and safety regulation ☑

Pollution emission regulations ☐

HMRC VAT rules ☑

Regulations over the export of goods ☐

Chapter 2

1   The correct answer is:

	Downward	**Upward**
Instructions	☑	☐
Exception reports	☐	☑
Briefings	☑	☐
Queries and questions	☐	☑
Plans	☑	☐
Routine reports	☐	☑
Decisions	☑	☐

2   The correct answer is: Office Manager

Because the relocation is being managed as a cross-functional project by the Office Manager, and this task specifically relates to the project (and not to your everyday work in the Accounts department), the person to report to here (in the first instance) will be the Office Manager.

3   The correct answer is: Accounts department where there are rarely any visits from non-employees

In an Accounts department where there are rarely any visits from non-employees, the employer may be happy for a degree of personalisation of work areas, eg the display of photographs. (However, these must be acceptable to others in the office, and create a professional appearance and environment.)

In a reception area open to the public or a Sales department where there are regular meetings with customers it will be important to give the right impression of the organisation. Therefore, in order to appear professional and efficient, there may be stricter rules regarding the amount of personalisation allowed in these areas.

4

Your supervisor asks you for details of the latest R&D expenditure on new products.

| Y |

A telephone caller, saying she is a financial journalist, asks you for details of your upcoming plans for new products.

| N |

A customer calls asking for the bank details of one of your fellow employees, stating that the customer wishes to pay a cheque into her bank account.

| N |

One of the senior accounts assistants has asked you to photocopy the notes for a training course that another rival company uses. You notice that the course notes have the copyright © symbol on them.

| N |

Explanations

The supervisor's request is a legitimate request from someone in a position of authority (provided that the R&D information is not flagged as 'classified', in which case authorisation may be required).

The telephone call request is likely to be sensitive information integral to the organisation's competitive advantage. Even if the caller is a journalist (and you have no way of knowing; she may be a competitor's R&D manager...), she has no right to this information, and should be politely refused.

Bank details are personal data (under the Data Protection Act) and should only be used for the purpose of making payments from the payroll. It is also highly personal and confidential information and should not be disclosed to anyone. The customer's request must be denied.

As the training course notes have the copyright symbol on them, they must not be photocopied without written permission from the copyright owner, the rival company. This must be explained to the senior accounts assistant and you should not copy them – unless permission has been obtained.

5   The correct answer is:

| Authorisations | are points in a procedure at which confirmation or permission to proceed must be obtained from an individual with appropriate authority.

| Designated signatories | are people who are authorised to sign documents (eg for authorisation purposes) or company cheques.

Chapter 3

1 | Feedback | is the response of a person with whom you are communicating, which indicates whether your message has (or has not) been received and understood as you intended.

Feedback is important in enabling you to adjust your message, if necessary, in order to ensure that the message has been received, and that there are no misunderstandings.

2   The correct answer is: £786.23

VAT in May = $\frac{20}{120}$ × £4,580 = £763.3333333 (rounded to £763.33)

VAT exclusive price in May = £4,580 – £763.33 = £3,816.67

There is a 3% increase in price for June so the VAT exclusive price in June will be:

£3,816.67 × 103% = £3,816.67 × 1.03 = £3,931.1701 (rounded to £3,931.17)

VAT on June purchase = £3,931.17 × 20% = £786.234 (rounded to £786.23)

3   The correct answer is: 26%

Percentage increase in revenue =

$$\frac{£20,916 - £16,600}{£16,600} \times 100 = \frac{£4,316}{£16,600} \times 100 = 0.26 \times 100 = 26\%$$

4   (a) Yours faithfully

(b) Yours sincerely

5   £635,000

Workings
Increase from 20X1 to 20X2 = 552,000 – 480,000 = 72,000. As a per cent this is 72,000/480,000 × 100 = 15%. 20X3 increase is 552,000 × 15% = 82,800. Add increase to 20X2 sales = 82,800 + 552,000 = 634,800. Nearest thousand = 635,000

Chapter 4

1   The correct answer is:

Situation	Method
Detailing a telephone message left by a supplier for a colleague	Informal note
Informing an employee that his work has not been up to standard recently	Face to face discussion*

Requesting a customer's sales ledger account balance from the credit controller	Email
Requesting production details for the last month from the factory manager where the factory is situated five miles away	Email
Sending monthly variances to the sales manager	Email

*A face to face discussion is necessary because of the sensitivity of the issue, and the need for interactive question and answer.

2   The correct answer is:

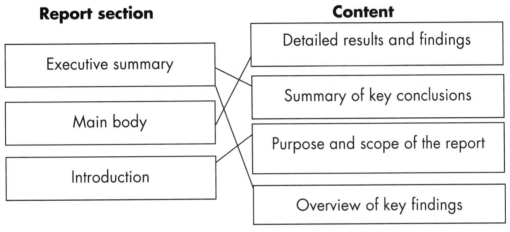

3

Your Name

Your Address

Jo Bloggs
3 Market Place
Shepherds Bush
London W12 1AW

[Today's Date]

Dear Jo,

The use of appendices in report writing

In response to your recent request for information about this, I thought you might appreciate the following key points.

The **purpose** of an appendix (or appendices) to a report is to separate out from the main body of the report any detailed data and supporting documents that might be helpful to the user, but might get in the way of the flow and conciseness of the main report.

In order to be used effectively, appendices should be limited in number, to avoid overloading the user with data. Each appendix should be numbered, and referred to clearly in the body of the report (eg 'see Appendix 1' or 'attached as Appendix 2'), so that the user can easily locate the supporting data if required.

These are very simple points, but I hope they are helpful to you.

If you want any further help with your report writing, just let me know. I'd be happy to help if I can.

Kind regards,

Your Name

4   (c)   *(note that verbs should all be in the same tense)*

5   (b)

6   (b)

Chapter 5

1   The correct answer is:

Task	Category
Preparing a petty cash summary by the end of next week	Not urgent but important
Packing up out of date files to be archived	Not urgent or important
Preparing a report for a meeting tomorrow	Urgent and important
Replenishing the milk in the kitchen this morning	Urgent but not important

2   The correct answer is:

A ⌐To Do list⌐ is a simple short-term planning tool and consists of a checklist listing the tasks that need completing for a particular day.

An ⌐action plan⌐ is a detailed planning tool which can be used for complex longer-term projects.

3   The correct answer is:

The latest date on which you could start work on this report is
⌐Friday 10 August⌐

	August							
	Fri 10	**Mon** 13	**Tue** 14	**Wed** 15	**Thu** 16	**Fri** 17	**Mon** 20	**Tue** 21
Req. files	X							
Research		X	X	X				
Analysis					X	X		
Typing							X	
Proofing								X

4

Action	✓
Carry on with the work, until completed at 5pm	
Report the delay to your manager	✓
Go home early without completing the payment run	
Start on one of tomorrow's tasks, and complete the payment run later	

5

Consequences	✓
A supplier is paid and the manager knows there are queries on the account.	✓
The bank rejects the BACS payment request for lack of signatures.	✓
The bank rejects the BACS payment request as it has not been authorised by the purchases ledger manager.	
Suppliers' payments are delayed.	✓

Chapter 6

1   The correct answer is:

Human resources team ☐

Inventory control section ☐

Payroll section ☑

Receivables ledger team ☑

2   Roles that people might occupy in a team will include:

Leading the team
Generating ideas
Implementing the ideas
Maintaining the relationships between the team members

3   It is highly likely that the tasks that you perform will have an effect on other team members. Information that you provide will be used by others and they may not be able to complete their tasks until you have completed yours. Therefore, schedules and timetables must be set by the team leader to ensure that there is full integration of the work of all team members. It is important that each individual meets their commitments according to the schedules set, in order for the team to achieve its objectives.

4   Synergy is the concept that sometimes two heads are better than one and therefore teams can often accomplish more than the same individuals working alone.

    Mutual assistance within teams can help provide synergies when one member of the team, still being able to fulfil their other commitments, is able to help another member struggling due to time or other restraints (for example lack of skill/experience in a particular area). This attitude is then reciprocated by the assisted team member when the roles are reversed.

    The overall result is that more work is completed on time and its quality is better than it may have otherwise been.

5   The correct answer is: Discuss your concerns with your colleague

    You should talk to the accounts assistant initially and explain your concerns. If there is no solution drawn from these discussions (and no improvement in the behaviour towards you), your only action would be to talk to your line manager about the problem.

6   **Win–lose**: one of you gets the file and the other doesn't. Result: one party fails to meet their commitments.

    Compromise: one of you gets the file now, and the other gets it later (although this has an element of win–lose, since the other has to work late or take it home). Result: commitments met, but perhaps personal dissatisfaction.

    Win–win: you photocopy the file and both take it – or one of you consults his/her boss and gets an extension of the deadline (since getting the job done in time is the real aim – not just getting the file). Result: both deadlines are met, and collaboration has probably enhanced the working relationship between the colleagues.

7   The correct answer is:

Sexual or racial harassment	✓
Unfair treatment or discrimination due to race, gender or disability	✓
Having to share a printer with another department	☐
An argument with a fellow employee over the tidiness of their workspace	☐

An employee being given an unfair workload ☑

An employee being blocked for promotion ☑

Chapter 7

1   Members of professional bodies are required to complete a certain amount of CPD as a condition of continuing membership. This ensures that their knowledge and skills are always up to date and of a good standard – which, in turn, protects the interests of their clients and employers, as well as the standing and credibility of the professional bodies and the accounting profession.

2   The correct answer is:

Enables improved job performance ☑

It saves time in the short term ☐

Potential for increased rewards and recognition ☑

Greater job security ☑

Decreased job satisfaction ☐

Valuable in the external job market ☑

Note that although learning and development will improve performance and save time in the long term, the time taken to undertake proper learning and development will mean the employee has less time to undertake other tasks in the short term.

3   Examples include (only four were required):

Courses	Internal or external educational or training courses
Journals/trade publications	Technical information and updates (and training/educational opportunities)
Books	Technical and educational material
Colleagues	Learning skills, methods and techniques from colleagues on a formal or informal basis
Observation	A method of learning by observing how colleagues or superiors carry out their tasks

4   Popular search engines are often used together with key words to find web pages with details of the laws and regulations you are looking for. However, those websites listed first may not be the most reliable websites if they are not provided by a recognised or reliable source. They may therefore not be up to date or may contain inaccuracies. This can have an impact on the individual using the information as they may rely on, or pass on, this incorrect information in their role as a professional.

In order to make sure the information being learned from is accurate, the integrity of the provider should be verified. Sometimes you are able to check the last date the page was updated to ensure it is up to date information and this should be checked wherever possible.

5   You can compare your own progress against your PDP goals on a regular basis. (Have you attained the targets you set?)

Another review method is to get informal feedback from your supervisor or colleagues. (How do they think you have improved – and could improve still further?)

Most organisations plan periodic progress reviews (especially in project work and for new recruits).

There will also probably be annual **performance appraisal** for all employees.

Chapter 8

1   The correct answer is:

	✓
True	
False	✓

Group values are very important, eg in families and friendship groups (which is where we get our ideas from), national cultures and organisations (which establish ethical norms and expectations by which we have to operate).

2   The correct answer is:

	✓
Enhance the reputation and standing of its members	✓
Limit the number of members that it has	
Make sure that its members are able to earn large salaries	

The AAT needs to protect its reputation and standing by maintaining standards of conduct and service among its members in order to be able to enhance the reputation and standing of its members (so that, for example, they are able to attract and retain clients).

3   The correct answer is:

	✓
Say that you will get back to him when you have looked up the answer.	
Give him the contact details of a friend in your firm who knows all about accounting standards.	
Clarify the limits of your expertise with the client.	✓

This is an issue of technical competence and due care. You should clarify the limits of your expertise with the client, and **then** seek information or guidance from the relevant source.

4   The correct answer is:

	✓
It is in the public interest that employees who fail to comply with standards are prosecuted.	
It is in the public interest that services are carried out to professional standards.	✓

5   The correct answer is:

	✓
Policies aimed at improving efficiency including reducing waste, using less energy and recycling	
A long-term programme involving a series of sustainable development practices aimed at improving organisational efficiency, stakeholder support and market edge	✓
A core part of an organisation's corporate social responsibility comprising efficiency, stakeholder support and market edge	

Bibliography

Adair, J. (2009) *Effective Time Management,* Basingstoke: Pan Macmillan.

Association of Accounting Technicians (2014) *AAT Code of Professional Ethics* [Online]. Available at: https://www.aat.org.uk/sites/default/files/assets/AAT_Code_of_Professional_Ethic s.pdf [Accessed 19 May 2017].

Covey, Stephen R. (1990) *The 7 Habits of Highly Effective People,* Simon & Schuster.

Data Protection Act 2018. (2018) London, TSO.

EU GDPR Portal. (2018). EU GDPR Information Portal. [online] Available at: https://www.eugdpr.org/ [Accessed 10 May 2018].

European Commission (2001) *Promoting a European Framework for Corporate Social Responsibility.* DOC/01/9. Brussels: Commission of the European Communities.

Foster Back, P. (2005) *Ethical Business Leadership,* London: Institute of Business Ethics.

World Commission on Environment and Development (1987) *Our Common Future,* New York: Oxford University Press.

Index

I

J

K

L

M

N

O

P

R

S

232

REVIEW FORM

How have you used this Course Book?
(Tick one box only)

☐ Self study

☐ On a course_____

☐ Other _____

Why did you decide to purchase this Course Book? *(Tick one box only)*

☐ Have used BPP materials in the past

☐ Recommendation by friend/colleague

☐ Recommendation by a college lecturer

☐ Saw advertising

☐ Other _____

During the past six months do you recall seeing/receiving either of the following?
(Tick as many boxes as are relevant)

☐ Our advertisement in Accounting Technician

☐ Our Publishing Catalogue

Which (if any) aspects of our advertising do you think are useful?
(Tick as many boxes as are relevant)

☐ Prices and publication dates of new editions

☐ Information on Course Book content

☐ Details of our free online offering

☐ None of the above

Your ratings, comments and suggestions would be appreciated on the following areas of this Course Book.

	Very useful	Useful	Not useful
Chapter overviews	☐	☐	☐
Introductory section	☐	☐	☐
Quality of explanations	☐	☐	☐
Illustrations	☐	☐	☐
Chapter activities	☐	☐	☐
Test your learning	☐	☐	☐
Keywords	☐	☐	☐

	Excellent	Good	Adequate	Poor
Overall opinion of this Course Book	☐	☐	☐	☐

Do you intend to continue using BPP Products?   ☐ Yes ☐ No

Please note any further comments and suggestions/errors on the reverse of this page. The BPP author of this edition can be emailed at: lmfeedback@bpp.com.

Alternatively, the Head of Programme of this edition can be emailed at: nisarahmed@bpp.com.

REVIEW FORM (continued)

TELL US WHAT YOU THINK

Please note any further comments and suggestions/errors below